SEE DESIGN • HEAR DESIGN • SPEAK DESIGN

SUPON DESIGN GROUP

ISBN 0-942604-87-3

Library of Congress Catalog Card Number 2001 135101

Distributed in North America to the trade and art markets by:
WATSON-GUPTILL PUBLICATIONS
770 Broadway
New York, NY 10003

Distributed throughout the rest of the world by:
HARPERCOLLINS INTERNATIONAL
10 East 53rd Street
New York, NY 10022

Published by:
MADISON SQUARE PRESS
10 East 23rd Street
New York, NY 10010

Printed in Hong Kong

SEE DESIGN • HEAR DESIGN • SPEAK DESIGN

ACKNOWLEDGMENTS

There are so many people I'd like to acknowledge and thank. Although they all work on behalf of me and the company I lead, they are the ones deserving of the credit our studio has earned. Their talent and passion for what they do are the true secrets to successful design. Teamwork is key—together we have raised the threshold for great design.

There are several individuals to whom I'd like to personally express my gratitude. First, I'd like to thank Jerry McConnell for your confidence in this project. Also, I must thank Ethan Assal, Julian Clopet, and Paul Duning of MHI for believing in me and my team. To Wayne Kurie, my friend, with whom I've had the privilege of working for over 14 years, you've been great. And to Pum Mek-aroonreung, who, as art director, spent countless hours on this book. Special thanks to Larry Olsen, lead photographer on this project, you've helped make our work shine. To my staff—past and present—with whom I've had the honor of working, I've enjoyed you all. And last, but certainly not least, I'd like to thank our clients for their trust and the meaningful relationships we've developed. I thank you all, from the bottom of my heart.

—Supon Phornirunlit

Project & Creative Director
SUPON PHORNIRUNLIT

Cover Designer
PUM MEK-AROONREUNG

Illustrator
JAE WEE

Book Designers
SCOTT BOYER
JENNIFER HIGGINS
LINDA LAM
SCOTT LIVINGSTON
KATE LYDON
PUM MEK-AROONREUNG
TODD METROKIN
MELISSA YACUK

Editors
CLARE JAMES
WAYNE KURIE

Lead Photographer
LAWRENCE OLSEN

Photographers
DEBBIE ACCAME
OI JAKARAT VEERASARN
SOMKID PAIMPIYACHAT

CONTENTS

GIVING MEANING,
AN INTRODUCTION

Throughout the course of time, regardless of culture, belief or origin, it seems that each generation has arrived at a simultaneously startling and comforting realization: A striking image can be more enduring and more effective than a spoken or written message alone.

Again and again, it is discovered that without the visual recognition that can accompany a message, our impression of it is often diminished. As graphic designers, we trust that this observation always holds true. But does a graphic image truly communicate better than just words? Can design be transmitted across all media, appealing to our senses and achieving a response in a way that words cannot? Can we see, hear and speak design?

Indeed, we can all draw a picture. Man has been drawing—albeit prehistoric renderings of bison on the walls of rock dwellings—since the beginning of the Middle Paleolithic period some 200,000 years ago.

But the task of today's designer goes beyond illustrating basic ideas and prehistoric concerns. It goes beyond creating pretty pictures and colorful typography, and beyond beefed-up graphics software. The designer's job demands that we push the boundaries of our individual creativity, manifesting our inventive notions to best fulfill our client's objective with a clear, unified message.

There is no question that graphic design is a powerful method of communication. Annual reports can inform, brochures can educate and packaging can persuade. How powerful is graphic design? It's in the hands of the designer. We pull the strings that compel the marionette to dance. We control a design's fate. Successfully transmitted message or misunderstood background noise? Every project is a fresh challenge, and with each one, we decide if design is seen, heard and spoken.

There are countless solutions to any design problem. Ask a design staff of twenty to create a logo for Corporation X, and you'll be handed twenty unique, innovative marks that meet the needs of the company. Some of the logos may look similar in chosen type face or color scheme, several may allude to Corporation X's industry or scope. But each of the twenty designers who began with the same basic information and raw materials will have used his or her individual creativity and vision to produce a concept that differs from every other in some way.

The thought of these twenty different logos is quite intriguing. The knowledge that multiple people can be given the exact same information about a project and produce vastly different results seems to validate the very purpose of a designer's trade. Indeed, it is likely that all of the designers came to their idea through virtually the same process: synthesizing information, brainstorming ideas, sketching those ideas and—with an often painstaking self-criticism and exploration—following the strongest through to its final form.

Every good designer is familiar with this challenge. In any project, we begin with only the raw materials—a sketchpad, pencils, an understanding of the client's problem. But with time and elements of energy, intelligence and creativity, we produce a completed piece that meets the client's expectations, solves the design problem and captures the essence of their vision in a graphic concept. This sense stems from good judgment and a thorough understanding and appreciation of a project. It suggests an artistic insight or vision, something beyond the creative that can't be learned—or taught—in a traditional way. This concept, this vision, is seeing design.

But what separates the good designs from the brilliant ones? The hallmark of brilliant design lies in its execution. Once sparked by the energy of inspiration, we find the path from concept to implementation is freed from obstacles and easier to follow. But where does the path end?

When do we add the last splash of color, the final illustrative stroke, the concluding word of copy? There is no absolute endpoint; no stop sign on the path. We must possess a sense that tells us when enough is enough. This sense, harmonizing execution and technique, is hearing design.

Even with the instinctual knowledge that our design is complete and any further additions would be detrimental, Corporation X may still have several strong concepts from which to choose. The group of candidates must then be refined further, as the Corporation considers which designs are appealing on personal, professional and visceral levels. Undoubtedly, all of the designs will be creative and unique, but one might be the seemingly obvious answer; so appropriate for the client that it's hard to imagine how they got along without it. The perfect fit. This ability, to make a design "fit" a company, is speaking design.

These are the choices that designers make and the skills we employ in the course of every project, whether annual report, poster or logo. As creative professionals, we recognize that graphic design is a valuable asset in today's business world—a discipline—not just a vehicle that decorates or embellishes. It conveys messages, gains and retains attention, appeals to global audiences and creates impressions.

However, the manifestation of our inventive notions on paper is no longer the only medium by which design concepts can be realized. Businesses have been using technology since the invention of the abacus, but the environment is rapidly evolving. Every day, more and more companies and organizations vie to reach their targeted audiences through dynamic new media. The novelty of the Internet—still in its infancy when compared with other time-tested methods of communication—poses a distinct marketing challenge for companies.

Internet business has become quotidian, and the speed and efficiency with which consumers can access content is paramount. As the vanguard of new directions in visual communications, the Internet has transformed the design landscape, reinventing the use of dynamic shapes, colors and forms. The culture of communication has changed, and as a result, design must now take on a dual purpose. It must be compelling yet functional, engaging yet versatile. The implementation of dynamic design and effective function requires a delicate balance that is difficult to achieve.

Whether print, broadcast, new media or something in between, the spectrum of design disciplines must coexist in a sea of innovation, with the graphic designer masterfully at the helm of digital technology. We must harness the power of the dot com medium to create unique visual communication solutions that firmly position our clients beyond the realm of traditional exposure. The challenge requires more strategic thinking, more problem-solving and more communication between designer and client. The result of these efforts, however, unifies traditional design and contemporary technology to create strong, memorable solutions that can communicate in ways heretofore unimaginable.

Indeed, it seems that strategies inherent in print and new media design have converged, uncovering a new world of possibilities for the graphic designer. Yet this junction of traditional and digital—the intersection of old and new—is not a complete departure from our past experiences and sensibilities. The values inherent in brilliant design remain unchanged, though the vehicles by which they are applied are more innovative. Ideas still matter. Sense, insight, vision and creativity still matter. These values—the signs of true excellence in design—continue to evolve at a pace that far outmatches that of the digital age.

This trend will likely continue well into the future. Digital technology will remain a significant tool for the craft of graphic design, just as design will remain as essential as marketing or advertising for the success of the technology industry. Perhaps thousands of years from now, as more highly evolved creatures teach, learn and live, they will look to this exciting age—this era of innovation—and recognize us as prehistoric pioneers in a time of revolutionary communication.

Perhaps they will applaud our efforts to transform information into interaction. Perhaps they will understand our creations that can transcend borders, languages and cultures. They will certainly recognize that, like themselves and the more primitive human race that came before us, the art of design is not confined to a medium, a style or a genre. It is confined only by that which we can understand, through clear, effective messages that communicate with our eyes, ears and mouths—and our hearts and minds.

The designer's job demands that we push the boundaries of our individual creativity, manifesting our inventive notions to best fulfill our client's objective with a clear, unified message.

SUPON DESIGN GROUP

A week at Supon Design Group amounts to a lot more than 40 hours. It involves more than 23 pots of coffee, 55 concept sketches and 197 active projects. In the first place, a week at Supon Design Group is often closer to 60 hours, but it is that which cannot be quantified that truly composes the studio.

In every minute of every hour at Supon Design Group there is progress. Whether chatting with a client, brainstorming with a colleague, researching in the library or experimenting with a technique, ideas are being communicated. Questions are posed, imaginations are explored, and solutions are discovered. • Within this environment of progress—this cradle of creativity—is a truly complex system. A collection of independent parts that function as a whole, it is a dynamic but stable landscape that balances the energies of producers and consumers. Designers and clients share relationships that thrive on diversity and make the most effective use of resources. Investments of time, energy and creativity yield useful products. • Success requires the discovery of a pleasing harmony, a rhythmic combination that is difficult to achieve. Like in nature, when inputs greatly exceed outputs the ecosystem can become stressed, resulting in pollution.

Like a small child whose quest for knowledge and desire to understand often pervades his every activity, Supon Design Group endeavors to know its clients—and their needs—intimately.

By contrast, if not enough time, energy and creativity are invested, the ecosystem can become impoverished. The lands must be continually fertilized. Minds must be stimulated and growth must be nurtured. Supon Design Group has thrived in these intense surroundings.

Perhaps the most powerful factor in its progress is the breadth of diversity that permeates the studio. A truly international staff, a global client base and a founder's quirky personality are evidence enough that this place is unique. Yet far below the surface, beneath the classic cookie jars that populate the shelves, Supon Design Group's diversity is embraced by staff and clients alike, fostering a creative spirit that cannot be produced or manufactured by a formula or machine.

It is in that same spirit that Supon Phornirunlit founded the firm in 1988. In the years since, the once uncertain venture has enjoyed remarkable success. A two-person project in a one-bedroom apartment has evolved into a 30-person graphic design team, housed in an expansive, full-service studio in the heart of Washington, D.C. In the process, Supon's led the firm to more than 1,000 national and international awards, including numerous best of show honors in print, new media, broadcast and packaging design.

For Supon, this transformation often still seems intangible. The journey from start-up to near instant recognition in industry circles is almost always fresh in his mind. In the studio, however, each week brings new challenges, new goals and new opportunities for discovery. Mondays begin

with a staff meeting. Senior designers showcase projects recently completed by the staff, highlighting in each what distinct lessons were learned and what clients were seeking. Did we achieve their objective? Are they happy? Are *we* happy? Nothing less than a whirlwind of activity follows. Client calls, research, brainstorming and sketches are followed by first drafts, second drafts, coffee and canines, then third drafts and fourth drafts— typically in the course of an afternoon. Deadlines are anticipated, budgets are respected, and communication goals are paramount. Projects range from corporate identities to annual reports to websites and back again, and clients arrive from across the street, across the river, across the ocean and beyond.

The studio considers its role in this process as one of both keen curiosity and valuable insight— an opportunity for growth, not just information-gathering. Like a small child whose quest for knowledge and desire to understand often pervades his every activity, Supon Design Group endeavors to know its clients—and their needs—intimately.

It is a process similar to when that inquisitive child reaches the dreaded stage in development in which every statement is peppered with questions of "Why?" However, Supon Design Group follows the "why?" with "who, what, when, where and how," ensuring that each client's design will fit its philosophy, goals and character.

Answers to these basic questions help establish design directions and objectives. Once confident with an overall knowledge of the client's business, the planning stage begins. Here, a child's ability to focus on a game, a puzzle or any engaging activity for hours at a time is reflected in Supon Design Group's approach. Preliminary brainstorms, ideas and sketches come in quick succession, as concepts are developed and initial reactions gauged. The design team works together in this process to produce a wide range of potential solutions—differing perspectives are encouraged. This yields more brainstorms, ideas and sketches, until the strongest and most appropriate are discovered.

Now the project becomes more focused and the core team of designers is refined. Designers have child-like license to color outside the lines, explore the limits of their creativity, and enjoy the beauty of bright colors and shapes. Such experimentation turns innovative ideas into concrete solutions. Client reaction is then sought. A close, constructive relationship, centered around open collaboration, ensures that feedback is understood and applied effectively. Here, the child's instruction to "play well with others" is heeded.

Eventually, the correct solution is found. What remains is to execute the project with the same energy, voracity and scrutiny that were poured into each previous step. Tight deadlines, small budgets and last-minute changes must be viewed as challenges, not obstacles.

In the end, success leads to a brief recess. Then Supon Design Group—never tired and never content—is back to another project, another process and another week.

MULTI-MEDIA HOLDINGS, INC.
www.mhiweb.com

Supon Design Group's April 1999 merger with Multi-Media Holdings, Inc. (MHI), allows the firm the opportunity to offer the services of a wide range of creative and marketing-oriented companies. MHI combines the talents of more than a dozen award-winning specialty agencies to create the East Coast's first large-scale, full-service integrated marketing communications agency. Multi-Media Holdings, Inc. can boast a distinctive approach to client service—and a distinctive clientele, including American Express, Celera Genomics, Compaq, Hughes, Microsoft, Nortel and Oracle. Combining insight and imagination with cost-effective strategy, MHI reaches beyond the capabilities of traditional agencies. Sixteen creative firms join together under its umbrella to form unique, multi-disciplinary teams that are customized to meet each client's needs and exceed its expectations.

With offices in the Washington, D.C. and Boston areas, MHI offers a broad expertise which encompasses strategic marketing, advertising, public relations, copywriting, database development, video and event staging, exhibit design, prepress services and commercial photography.

MHI's unique approach—providing a wealth of creative and production services to clients from within one resource-rich environment—is reflected in its philosophy. MHI offers clients integrated marketing from print to .com™. Each a smaller piece of the whole, the agency's individual firms all work together to meet the needs of clients.

Whether chatting with a client, brainstorming with a colleague, researching in the library or experimenting with a technique, ideas are being communicated.

AT YOUR SERVICE

This balancing act is not easy to sustain.

"Businesses planned for service are apt to succeed; businesses planned for profit are apt to fail."

When educator and Columbia University president Nicholas Murray Butler spoke these words near the beginning of the twentieth century, he could not have known how right he was.

Today, "service industries" account for more than two-thirds of the gross national product and employment of developed countries. From tourism and entertainment to retail and finance, the impact of this rapidly growing economic area is also being felt in developing countries.

The professional service industry accounts for more than a quarter of all U.S. jobs. Whether specializing in public relations, marketing, advertising, law or graphic design, these companies are charged with the task of providing a service to a client, creatively solving their problem while influencing the attitudes and behavior of targeted audiences.

The biggest challenge these companies face is simultaneously cultivating and maintaining relationships with two very distinct groups: the client and the audience. While they must strive to clearly communicate the client's message to a targeted audience, they must also be ever-vigilant for how they convey these messages, ensuring accuracy and efficacy at all times.

This balancing act is not easy to sustain. Companies must send messages designed to inform, persuade or educate the public about their clients' products, services or ideas. They must also inspire trust and honesty from their public. A daunting enough challenge, professional service companies must develop their own identities, conveying responsibility, professionalism and know-how.

These companies must effectively communicate their own services before they can communicate on behalf of their clients. By establishing a niche in their respective fields and using the power of graphic innovation, the following companies have adopted design themes that show they planned for service, and are succeeding because of it.

MANNINGTON COMMERCIAL

When Mannington Commercial decided to update its identity and packaging system, it sought a distinct design solution that would reflect the durable quality and contemporary appearance of its carpet, sheet flooring and tile products. In short, it wanted a concept that would stand out and defy convention.

Since 1915, Mannington Mills has remained steadfast in its goal: To serve as the only flooring company in the United States to offer consumers carpet, sheet flooring, tile, wood and laminate products from a single source. • Mannington's commitment to its vision of "One Source, Many Solutions" allows the company to provide its clients with progressive, affordable products that combine style and performance to coordinate beautifully in virtually any environment. • The company's flooring products have been regularly awarded and named among the best by some of the most prestigious interior design firms and retailers in the country. Mannington is also dedicated to quality control standards that lead the industry, holding numerous patents for equipment improvement and innovation. A division of Mannington Mills, Mannington Commercial echoes these commitments. • Marketing to

SALUKI (SALU)

IMARI (IMAR)

KEARNEY (KEAR)

LARKIN (LARK)

HIGHGROVE (HIGR)

FLETCHER (FLET)

architects and interior designers, rather than directly to consumers, Mannington Commercial faced a unique design challenge when it decided to update its sales and marketing system. The company wanted a distinct design solution that would reflect the durable quality and contemporary appearance of its carpet, sheet flooring and tile.

More importantly, however, it felt it needed to make a dramatic departure from the conventional, plain black-and-white avenues often taken by its competitors. It sought an alternative packaging concept: one that would distinguish Mannington Commercial in the marketplace and appeal to a very design-savvy audience. It wanted to make a memorable impression, communicating its mission and reflecting its commitment to quality

and service. In short, Mannington Commercial wanted a concept that would stand out and defy convention.

The solution was an exciting new corporate identity based on vibrant color and illustration, united by a set of guidelines establishing how the various graphic elements should be combined. In this way, images and type work within a consistent system to obtain maximum visual impact from one medium to the next.

The foundation of the new identity is a customized color palette, which consists of 10 color schemes. Three colors work in concert to create each of the 10 schemes. Each Mannington Commercial product line, whether carpet, vinyl tile or sheet

Mannington Commercial's corporate materials incorporate various elements of its packaging system, while the library of sample folders virtually leaps off the shelves of interior designers and architects.

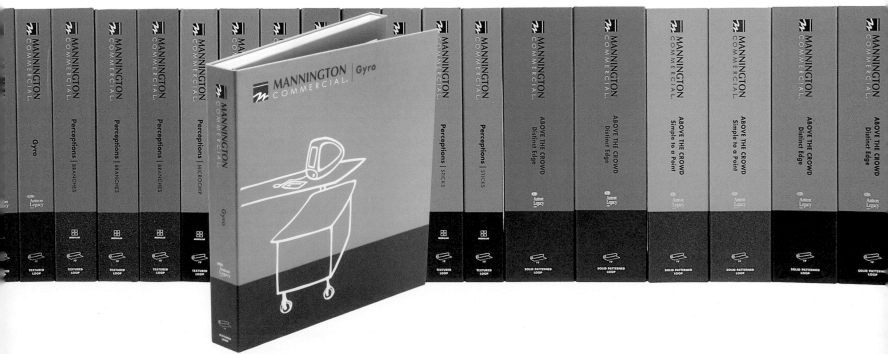

flooring, follows an associated color scheme. As a result, each product line can be autonomous for presentation kits and promotional materials, but all remain a consistent part of the larger Mannington Commercial identity.

Equally as important to the success of Mannington's new identity was the development of an illustration library, featuring dozens of customized drawings of classically modern furniture. When applied to folders and notebooks, the subtlety of hand-drawn line art doesn't take away from the product, but in fact accentuates its integration with other elements in a room. Colored in bright shades of yellow, red and blue, the illustrations bring together the radically different approach

Mannington was seeking with a visually functional demonstration of its products.

The company adapted this branding approach across various applications, maintaining consistency overall while remaining versatile enough to accommodate any need. To further distinguish between its products, the carpet, tile and sheet flooring architect folders were each given distinct appearances—while still following the established color and illustration systems. To reflect the look and feel of each product, the carpet folders have a soft edge with a dull finish, while the tile folders depict a checkerboard design on a high-gloss finish. Such attention to detail is a key element of the identity.

The sales kit reflects the varied elements of Mannington Commercial's new packaging system, seamlessly combining color schemes and illustrations into a format that can stand alone or work together with other materials.

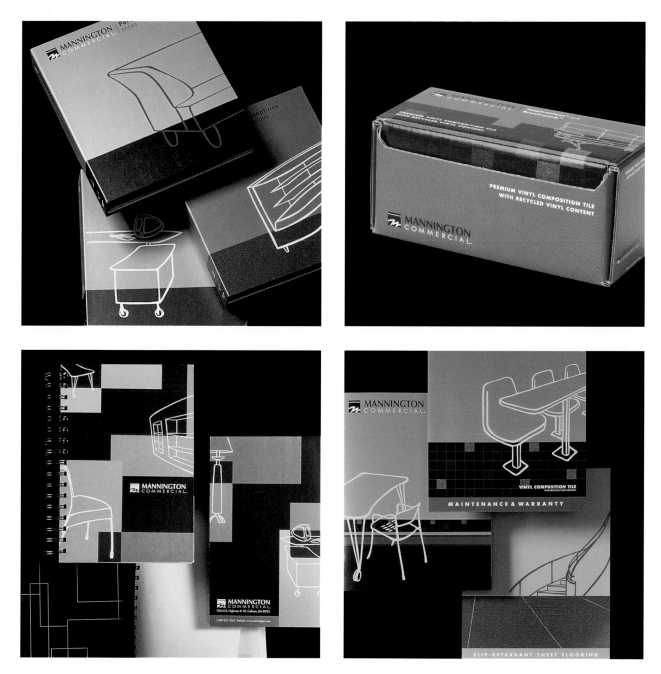

LEFT TO RIGHT: Carpet swatch folders, vinyl tile sample box, promotional notebook, various publications. Mannington's packaging system is designed to accommodate a variety of marketing needs while retaining overall visual consistency.

Packaging for Mannington's Design Line holds samples of top-of-the-line, customized carpet created for commercial clients. Mannington's corporate accounts materials employ a professional two-color scheme, but feature modern illustrations selected from its hand-drawn library, a portion of which is shown at right.

When it came time to design collateral materials that were not product specific, it made sense to incorporate the various colors and illustrations into one separate, organized structure all its own. The sales kits, folders and notebooks convey this approach, as simple squares are imbued with the energy contained in 10 color schemes and varied illustrations. The result proves that the numerous elements of Mannington Commercial's identity do in fact work in harmony.

Mannington Commercial's new packaging system easily stands apart from competitors' and nearly leaps off the shelves of interior designers and

architects. The bright color palette and corresponding elements counter traditional expectations of a commercial flooring company. From swatch books and presentation kits to promotional materials and collateral pieces, the company's printed identity is fresh and confident.

Along with the graphic standards that guide their use, the new packaging designs ensure a unified image that is easily recognizable and professional. Using materials that are both technically effective and visually innovative, the company succeeds in communicating its messages and demonstrating the value of its products.

  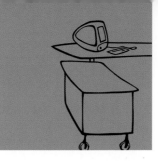  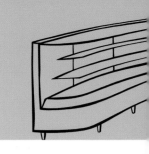

 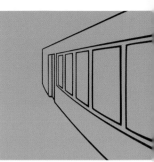

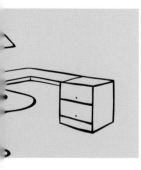 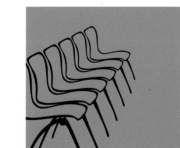  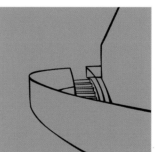 

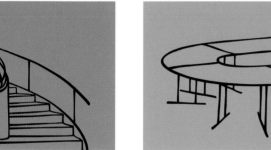 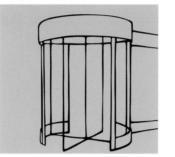   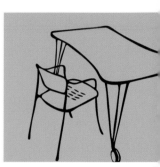

 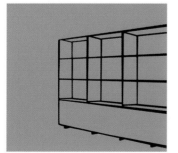 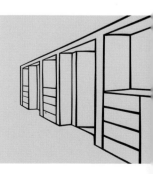

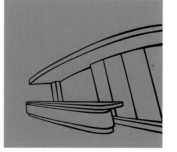 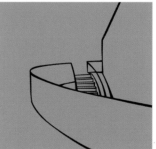 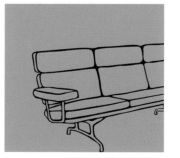

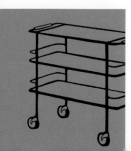 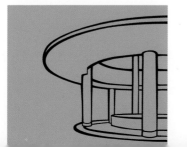   

CPI Restoration A new face in exterior building restoration needed a strong marketing presence to establish its identity. A statue of a lion is reminiscent of classical architecture—an appropriate logo for a company which restores older buildings to their former glory. The brochure speaks volumes, but is also an effective visual tool to introduce the company and its services.

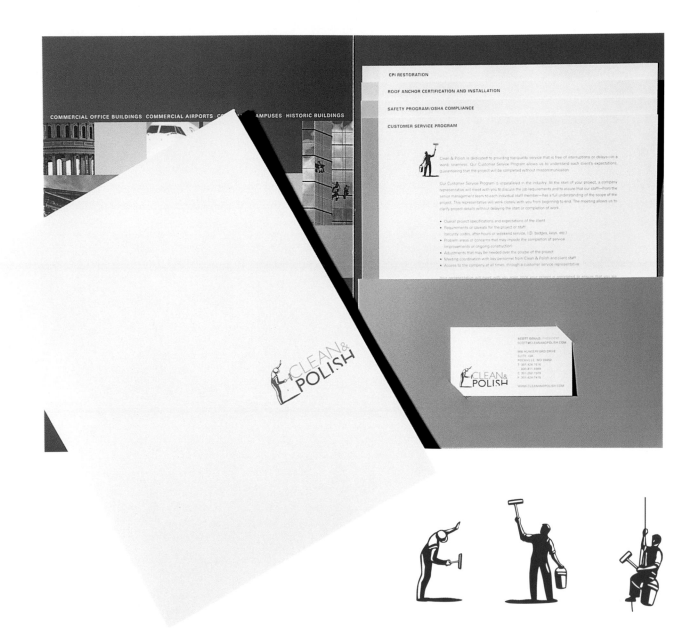

Clean & Polish **Playful, yet serious marks form the basis of an identity that conveys this commercial and industrial building maintenance company's broad range of services, as well as its experience and professionalism.**

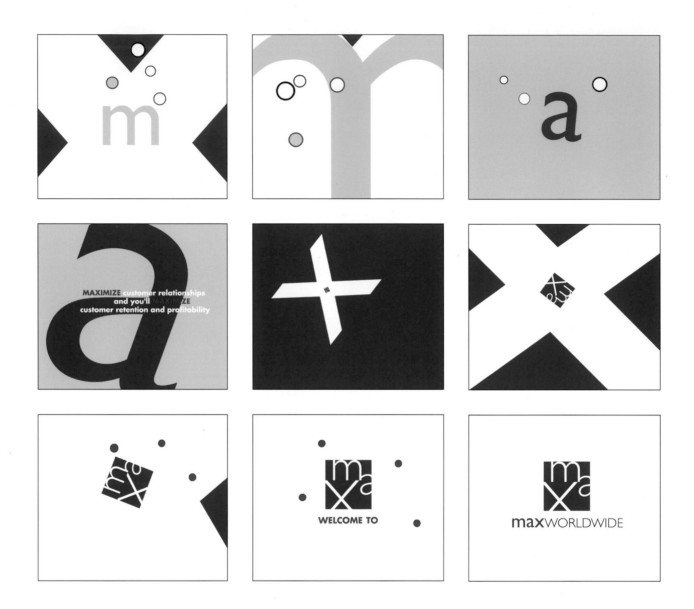

MAXWorldwide A professional but playful, self-assured but daring logo was elaborated upon for MAXWorldwide's website animation. A marketing and consulting company that develops customer loyalty strategies and programs for businesses, the visual identity for MAXWorldwide communicates that its approach is fresh, unexpected, progressive but—most importantly—memorable.

Hai Finance Corporation The print materials for this investment company reflect the dynamic industries and innovative enterprises that it targets. Bold, technology-driven graphics, an imaginative color palette and compelling shout-out keywords combine to give these pieces a cutting-edge look that communicates a sense of urgency and opportunity for potential investors.

This firm's unique approach to client service is reflected in its marketing materials. As represented by a square composed of many smaller squares, MHI's individual firms work together to meet client needs. On a simple, professional blue background, the logo is extended to capabilities brochures, packaging and collateral materials.

MHi
MULTI-MEDIA HOLDINGS, INC.

1730 M ST. NW | SUITE 600 | WASHINGTON | DC 20036 | T. 202.835.3000 | F. 202.835.2022

Relentless Service: From Top to Bottom
Working as a Team to Meet Your Goals

We've seen it a hundred times before: A big agency comes in with all the rainmakers. But when it's time to do the work, they send in the junior staffers.

At MHI, you work with senior-level marketing strategists, creatives, and researchers. Seasoned people with a couple of decades of experience under their belts. In fact, they're MHI shareholders, so they're not just committed to serving clients. They're relentless. And they won't stop until you get the results you need.

Flexibility is the key — As an MHI client, your account team is built in whatever way makes the most sense for you. There's no formula, because each account team is built specifically around your business needs. This team could include an account executive, creative director, online marketing analyst, media planner, and project manager. It might include several senior creative directors. Or experts in marketing to several different targets. We're flexible, and we reconfigure our operating style around you.

"We feel a strong sense of partnership with MHI. Their responsiveness and ability to understand our market have been great assets as we've launched marketing programs to both internal and external customers. Without a doubt, we're a stronger company because of our relationship with MHI."

ROB MOORHEAD
Vice President, Marketing

MHI gives you vast resources. With facilities in Washington, D.C., Maryland, and Northern Virginia, MHI is comprised of more than 50 of the most committed, creative people in the business.

To ensure complete control over our creative product, we run our own prepress production facilities, photo labs, and on-demand digital printing operations. Our own video production studio includes complete event staging capabilities. We even have a fully-equipped exhibit showroom to help you choose your next trade show structure.

Marketing Collateral

Integration is key in developing successful marketing campaigns — not only is message, but in process and execution alike. A message that is repeated across numerous publications or communicating materials is one that is more likely to be remembered. But for that to happen, detailed coordination among those producing the communicating materials is paramount. This assures that the initial design and content is neither diluted nor altered as it's applied from piece to piece over time.

Associated Press: In celebration of AP's 150th anniversary, a fully branded identity was developed that suggested the past, present, and future of the respected news organization. This identity included print items such as stationery, folders, and brochures as well as specialty items such as neckties and banners. A special web site link was also created in support of the celebration.

Ovación: This presentation package was designed to promote Ovación's unique programming and to encourage cable operators throughout Latin America to add the channel to their lineups. The kit contains an oversized booklet featuring lively images of the programming and an accompanying video. Photos of performers, paintings, sculpture, and concerts highlight the package.

CSX intermodal: CSX needed a communications strategy to provide customers with reference information about its transportation services. The result was an accessible and expandable ring-binder system with a series of informational brochures. Each brochure could also be used separately to respond to customer requests for specific information.

The George Washington University: These undergraduate recruiting materials featured a bold, aggressive look, aimed at appealing to 16- and 17-year old high school students. As a result of this departure from the University's previous marketing identity, the number of applications for admission rose dramatically.

IBM: IBM's sponsorship of the Summer Olympic Games in Atlanta prompted the creation of a new brand identity in honor of the occasion. The identity cleverly utilizes IBM's familiar blue bands, but in a novel way, with individual applications ranging from as small as a collector's pin to as large as a bus wrap.

INTEGRATED MARKETING

WARDS The perfect combination of sentiment and practicality was necessary to communicate the philosophy of an organization supporting the professional care of animals in research. Its logo clearly emphasizes compassion, illustrating a caring relationship and response between humans and animals.

Alexander Street Press Historic research on subjects as diverse as the American Civil War and early exploration and discovery are available from Alexander Street in CD or magnetic tape format. As content primarily comes from old letters and other personal accounts, promotions are richly layered in imagery of handwritten diaries and photos.

Oldcastle Materials Group Dublin-based Oldcastle is a federation of architectural-product companies that retain their local identities and autonomy while leveraging the strength of the larger group. Aiming to attract new companies to become part of the federation, the site visually illustrates the benefits of collaboration and collective influence.

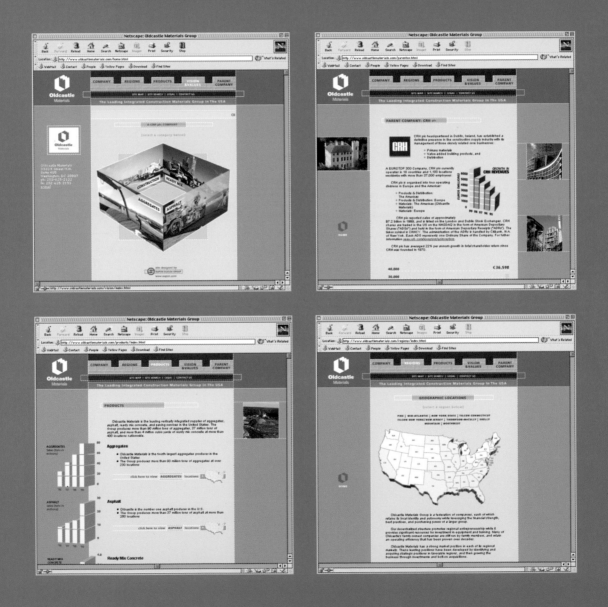

LEFT TO RIGHT: **HortiCare, landscape design firm; Linda Klinger, writer and editor; Louise Owen III, watchmaker; BrandHarvest, strategic branding and marketing firm; e-satisfy, customer satisfaction measurement company; City Optical, optical shop.**

EMM How could EMM link its name with its advertising, branding and marketing services in the minds of potential clients? A marketing kit that capitalizes on clever word play and bold, solid colors and graphics fits the bill. Custom packaging houses a wire-bound promotional brochure, CD and video. Anyone who receives this unique self-promotion will be hard pressed not to open it.

CJ Group The stationery created for this consulting firm is a refreshing break from the conservative designs often seen in the industry. Signifying the owner's daughter, as well as the firm's strategic thinking, the "C" plays off the "thought bubble" concept to offer a creative twist to a straightforward design problem.

OPPOSITE: **Madison Square Press, Books Nippan, Rockport Publishers** Whether logo creation or publication design, breaking the rules or sticking to a budget, these books—about design and by designers—are in a class of their own. For those hesitant to judge a book by its cover, every page is a refreshing visual delight.

Abbeville Press Do the letters of a name or the numbers of a birth date hold secrets to people's personalities? This fun-filled novelty book says they do. Delightful illustrations, fanciful calligraphy and a light-hearted design that doesn't take itself too seriously distinguish this book from others in its genre. Tabs, wheels and windows make *What's in a Number?* fun and interactive.

Debbie Accame A graceful, sweeping logo highlights the identity for photographer Debbie Accame. On the website's homepage, this icon is applied to a colorful, complex texture which almost gives the impression of a watercolor painting. At the same time, though, the primary focus of the site is Debbie's portfolio.

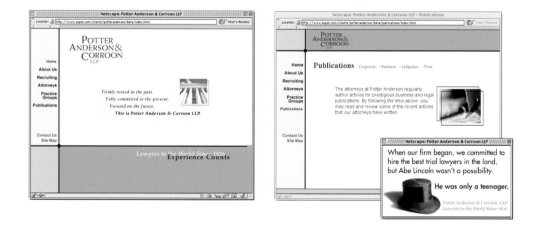

Potter Anderson & Corroon This well-established law firm recognized that its website was an important tool for representing itself to the public. The site was redesigned to convey a more sophisticated and up-to-date image. Balancing content-rich pages with a professional, uncluttered layout, the firm's image resonates with current and prospective clients.

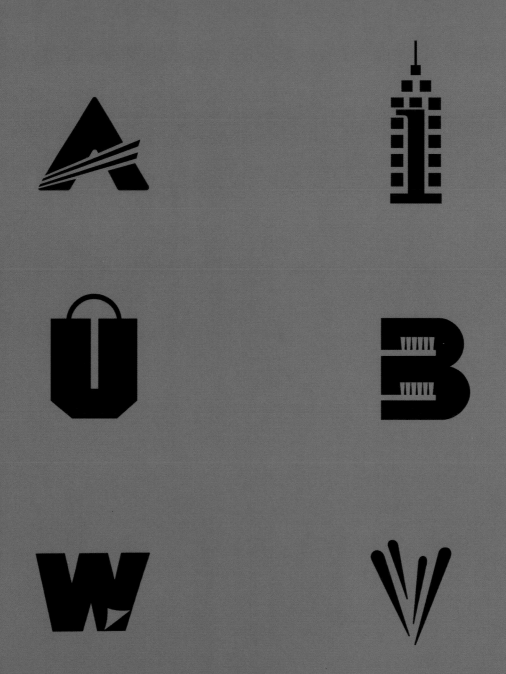

LEFT TO RIGHT: Adventist Healthcare Mid-Atlantic, hospital consortium; Building One, building facilities services company; Ulman Paper Bag Company, bag manufacturer; Steven T. Bunn, DDS, dentist; Walsh Wallpaper Company, wallpaper installer; Virginia Hospital Center, hospital and health care facility.

Pace An energy services company, Pace is given a whole new stage when its revolving-Earth logo is enlarged and die-cut from the cover of its annual report. A fly sheet is printed in swirling, illuminated hues—the perfect backdrop to introduce the use of graphic photography featuring energy sources.

Your Energy Trustee℠

Clients have the option of hiring us to perform individual consulting tasks or they may choose to have us integrate a suite of services into a comprehensive *Energy Trustee℠* program. Pace's *Energy Trustee℠* program establishes a framework for identifying and exploiting cost-reduction opportunities while providing expert energy portfolio management. From competitive procurement of fuels and power, to load aggregation, to ongoing transactional management, Pace applies a total-systems perspective to help clients extract the full value of their corporate-wide energy assets and transactions.

The *Energy Trustee℠* concept is predicated on Pace's ability to work with clients as an invaluable extension of their in-house energy staff. We combine our energy expertise with a firm understanding of each client's unique corporate culture to ensure that all program recommendations fit within the client's broader business objectives. By working with Pace to develop a custom-tailored *Energy Trustee℠* program, clients can devote more time to their core business, secure in the knowledge that all their energy needs are being met by an objective outsourcing partner.

PACE'S ENERGY TRUSTEE℠ PROGRAM ESTABLISHES A FRAMEWORK FOR IDENTIFYING AND EXPLOITING COST-REDUCTION OPPORTUNITIES WHILE PROVIDING EXPERT ENERGY PORTFOLIO MANAGEMENT."

PACE | Global Energy Services

Setting the PACE in Energy

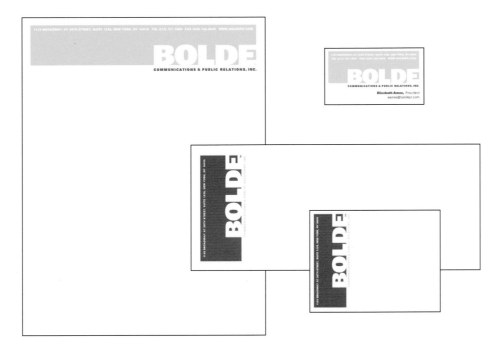

BOLDE A communications and public relations agency known for its exceptional service, BOLDE's design approach needed to reflect its name—strong and powerful, yet simple and even edgy. Deep gold and gray tones are a departure from expected colors and a bright and sophisticated addition to a truly "bold" identity.

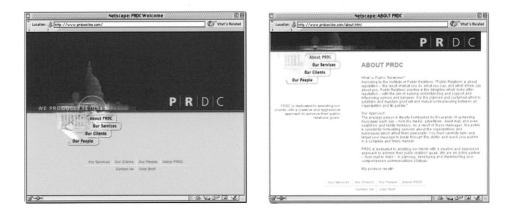

PRDC A catchy, to-the-point name steered the look of both the print and online identities for this full-service Washington, D.C., public relations firm. The logo is bold and memorable and the website is clean—almost sleek—but very professional. The site's template format makes regular updating a breeze.

CAUSE & EFFECT

Buy more cotton shirts. Drive safely.
Support medical research.

Cotton and cars. Research and restaurants. Whales and women's rights.

What do they have in common? Not much, except that there is an organization to represent each one. And just about everything else you can think of. For the most part, these organizations aren't typically in the spotlight—but all that's changing.

Whatever the focus, associations, foundations and institutions play an intrinsic role in each of our lives—working to change or improve our society by motivating us to action. Buy more cotton shirts. Drive safely. Support medical research. Eat restaurant food. Save the whales. Fight for gender equality.

Virtually every industry, cause and interest has a representative organization that raises public awareness and promotes its vision. Whether locally, regionally or internationally, these organizations strive to educate and inform their audiences in an effort to achieve their goals.

Most associations, foundations and institutions provide their members with educational materials and programs. Businesses and governments worldwide look to them for research and statistics concerning a particular cause or industry. They spend billions each year on books, periodicals, newsletters and websites. As a result, they demand design that encapsulates their missions, goals and efforts in a creative visual identity.

Designers must create solutions for the variety of printed and online materials each organization produces. Each design concept must adequately convey a sense of growth and purpose. It must clearly and effectively communicate a message, persuading readers to join the cause and take action within their communities and beyond. It must present the organization as an invaluable resource and a strong leader. It must achieve all of this through the use of color, typography and imagery.

Throughout the next few pages are examples of design that successfully meet each of these challenges. From printed brochures and reports to websites, the featured organizations use design savvy to highlight their good works and communicate their value to their targeted audiences. With the help of powerful design, these organizations may all one day achieve their goals—whatever their industries.

NEWSPAPER ASSOCIATION
OF AMERICA

The Newspaper Association of America's extensive design needs not only required creative graphics, but efficient management as well. The challenge was to convey a robust and optimistic image for the industry while addressing critical marketing objectives.

What's black and white and read all over? As more Americans "dot com" through each day, one might think that it would be more difficult to solve this age-old riddle. One might think that newspapers and other traditional media outlets would feel the impact of the Internet's arrival. Ironically though, one might be wrong. • Newspapers—the oldest form of today's popular media—remain the only news source used regularly by all types of audiences. At once tangible and ephemeral, they can be picked up, read in multiple sittings or all at once and tucked away neatly during transit; but they can also be thrown out and renewed tomorrow for very little investment. This is the power of newspapers. But in a media landscape that is more fragmented than ever, it takes a wealth of information, insight and innovation to stay ahead. • In addition to the Internet,

"Opportunity Knocks Again!" drives real estate agents' excitement about advertising in newspapers. With priceless research and statistics, each element of the kit is a valuable tool in helping advertisers reach out to consumers. NAA's annual report features rich colors and warm photographs.

magazines, television and radio also vie for consumers' attention—in an environment in which Americans often have considerably less time to follow the news. As a result, reliable branding strategies have become indispensable tools for newspapers to maintain a competitive edge.

The Newspaper Association of America represents the interests and promotes the success of thousands of newspapers across the country. With such a huge membership and broad agenda, the organization produces hundreds of publications each year, all designed to improve newspapers' bottom line.

NAA recognized that its members had to perceive the organization as an invaluable part of the industry. Its visual image had to project a distinctive and attractive corporate style. It had to build positive perceptions—both by members of other media and its own—of all of its publications and promotions, collateral materials and marketing tools.

NAA's extensive design needs not only required creative graphics, but efficient management as well. The challenge was to convey a robust and optimistic image for the industry while addressing critical marketing objectives. The goal was to revamp the image of newspapers, while communicating NAA's key goals with compelling visual treatments.

From campaigns that encourage newspaper advertising to programs that promote the needs of the industry, NAA's various brochures, annual

NAA's resources for political advertising in newspapers take on a clearly bipartisan approach—but employ strong imagery symbolizing both parties to inspire a real sense of competition and motivation for readers. A departure from typical direct mail promotions, humorous postcards use kitschy copy and retro black-and-white photos to alert newspaper executives to valuable management and development tools available from NAA.

reports, direct mail pieces—even holiday cards and product packaging—all take on a distinct creative identity, but communicate clear and interconnected messages that stress the organization's commitment to reinforcing newspapers' strong influence in society.

One such campaign sponsored by NAA is the annual ATHENA awards banquet, honoring creativity in newspaper advertising. The competition draws a vast array of entries, from traditional ads to public service announcements, but all have one thread of commonality— placement in newspapers.

For the most recent ATHENA, a deck of cards accompanied each invitation to the event, appropriately themed "The Magic of the Creative." Featuring ATHENA aces and jokers that playfully depict the hosts—magicians Penn & Teller—the deck of cards is a charming, engaging giveaway. The invitation even details instructions for a card trick. In both, old-style illustration works together with punchy, tongue-in-cheek copy to assure the pieces are guaranteed keepsakes for all invitees.

NAA's annual report, by contrast, takes a clearly different approach. The document contains a second report within its back-pocket folder, detailing the contributions of NAA's foundation

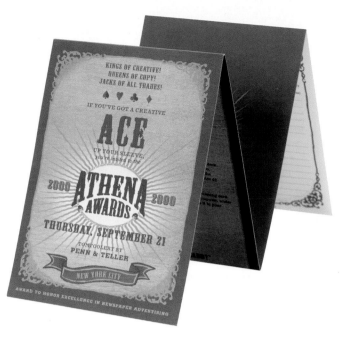

A practical deck of cards accompanied every magic-themed invitation to the most recent ATHENA (Awards to Honor Excellence in Newspaper Advertising) banquet. Combining humorous illustration and witty copy, the pieces are keepsakes for all invitees.

to charities and children's literacy programs. The two separate pieces are tied together by a richly hued red-and-gold color scheme and warm photographs and illustrations. The images appeal to the emotions and reflect the influence newspapers can have. With the necessary financial information in the back of each report, the two booklets also function as promotional materials that can be used throughout the year.

In another promotion, a package geared toward real estate agencies and advertisers presents vital research in a way that demonstrates the benefits of communicating with consumers via newspaper ads. Sales guides, newspaper studies, key findings and selling tools are all collected in a box, along

with a CD-ROM and packages of brochures that can be distributed to both colleagues and customers. The playful village graphics emphasize newspapers' ubiquity in the community, while the kit's layout unites information in one cohesive unit.

With a centralized creative process and a strong brand to present its goals and issues, NAA's various marketing pieces ensure that newspapers retain their vital role in the media mix. In an industry of opportunity—of adaptability—NAA has rebuilt itself into an organization that doesn't just react to changes in its environment, but drives them. It is well positioned as a key contributor in a new marketplace filled with choices.

www.apa.org/ads/ratecard

MEDIA PLANNING GUIDE

AMERICAN
PSYCHOLOGICAL
ASSOCIATION

Discover the Power of A

ADV

AMERICAN
PSYCHOLOGICAL
ASSOCIATION

CARD No. 32

ADVERTISING RATE

AMERICAN
PSYCHOLOGICAL
ASSOCIATION

CARD No. 33

OPPOSITE: American Psychological Association **The bright, friendly design featured throughout APA's media planning guide for advertisers engenders an accessible, inviting feel on every page. A combination of hand-drawn faces and vibrant nature photographs makes the design flexible and down-to-earth, while the layout of the brochure organizes all the relevant information.**

American Society of Interior Designers **ASID's monthly magazine, Access, was in need of a new look. In addition to redesigning the publication, a full set of graphic standards for future editions was created. This new, more contemporary guise is befitting an industry whose mission is effective design with strong aesthetics.**

Art Directors Club of Metropolitan Washington The identity for the Art Directors Club of Metropolitan Washington had to be both innovative and inexpensive to produce. Black-and-white photos of Washington landmarks—such as the Jefferson Memorial and National Cathedral—were subjected to several generations of photocopying to produce a unique distressed look.

LEFT TO RIGHT: **National Italian American Foundation, Italian-American advocacy organization; National Center for Family Philanthropy, organization advocating and facilitating philanthropic giving; International Food Policy Research Institute, agricultural policy aid organization; Connect for Kids, community improvement program; People For the American Way, civil rights advocacy organization; Association for the Care of Children's Health, The Campaign For Kids and Families.**

From the telegra...

the human story, a tale of everyday drama and histo...

In this 150th anniversary year, the men and women of the AP

carry on its proud tradition of journalistic excellence, committed to

ensuring its news remains fair, accurate and impartial.

Associated Press As the oldest and largest news organization in the world, the Associated Press required an appropriately unique and appropriate identity for its 150th anniversary. The "AP 150" campaign incorporates AP's existing logo into commemorative pieces that feature the organization's Pulitzer Prize-winning photography. Three consecutive annual reports (below) adapt this treatment.

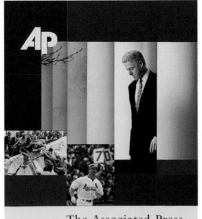

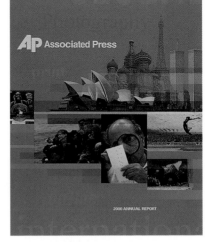

the american institute of architects 2001

honor awards

CELEBRATING THE BEST IN CONTEMPORARY ARCHITECTURE

the architecture

twenty-five interiors

year award urban design

AIA

THE SMITH HOUSE. ARCHITECT: RICHARD MEIER & PARTNERS. PHOTOGRAPHER: EZRA STOLLER AND SCOTT FRANCES/ESTO

OPPOSITE: **American Institute of Architects** Rather than a typical call for entries, the AIA commissioned a poster that would appeal to architects' design sensibilities and generate interest in its honor awards. Attractive enough to be hung on the wall, the poster features the previous year's winner on the front, with a full entry form on the reverse.

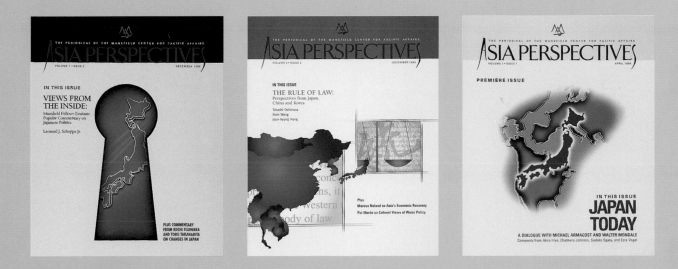

The Mansfield Center for Pacific Affairs A foundation dedicated to advancing relations between the United States and Asia, The Mansfield Center publishes a monthly magazine for its members entitled *Asia Perspectives*. A clean, simple layout directs readers' attention to articles exploring politics, business, education, foreign affairs and social issues.

District of Columbia Jewish Community Center Lively, colorful banners communicate the JCC's wide variety of recreational, social and intellectual activities. Whether viewed by teenagers or adults, Jews or gentiles, these banners quickly and dynamically convey that everyone is welcome at "The 16th Street J."

Broadcast Designers Association Award-winning projects from BDA's annual design competition are featured in this hardcover publication. As the book's market is heavily comprised of members of various creative industries, the challenge was to design a publication that was fresh and unique in itself, but did not take away from the featured work.

World Bank Presented at a European conference to raise awareness of the World Bank's programs addressing the needs of children around the world, this magazine uses powerful photography, unified by a bright color palette, to reach its readers.

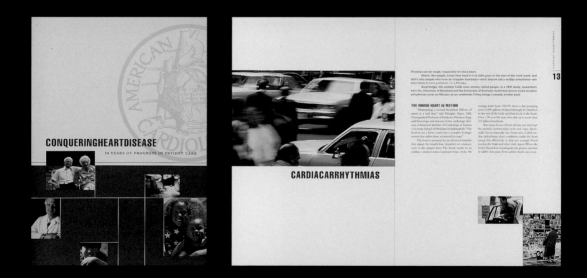

American College of Cardiology This publication was designed with patients' needs in mind. Produced by the ACC and available in doctors' waiting rooms, the articles are narrated by victims of heart disease and written for the everyday consumer.

NATIONAL CENTER JOURNAL
VOLUME 1

RESOURCES *for* FAMILY PHILANTHROPY

FINDING THE *BEST PEOPLE*, ADVICE, AND SUPPORT

NATIONAL CENTER
FOR FAMILY
PHILANTHROPY

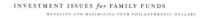

NATIONAL CENTER JOURNAL
VOLUME 2

INVESTMENT ISSUES *for* FAMILY FUNDS

MANAGING AND MAXIMIZING YOUR PHILANTHROPIC DOLLARS

NATIONAL CENTER
FOR FAMILY
PHILANTHROPY

NATIONAL CENTER JOURNAL
VOLUME 3

DONOR LEGACY

THE VALUES OF A FAMILY'S PHILANTHROPY ACROSS GENERATIONS

NATIONAL CENTER
FOR FAMILY
PHILANTHROPY

NATIONAL CENTER JOURNAL
VOLUME 4

FAITH *and* FAMILY PHILANTHROPY

NATIONAL CENTER
FOR FAMILY
PHILANTHROPY

National Center for Family Philanthropy NCFP not only encourages charitable giving, but helps donors throughout the process, with numerous workbooks, manuals and guides. It wanted a consistent, elegant look for these pieces that would appeal to its sophisticated audience.

National Cable Television Association Promoting its role as "Cable's Education Connection," this brochure highlights the events and programs NCTA—and its many cable system and cable network members—sponsors in schools around the country. Bold colors and a youth-oriented approach demonstrate that cable TV is indeed worth watching.

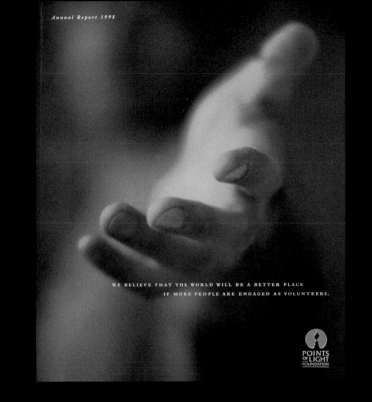

Annual Report 1998

WE BELIEVE THAT THE WORLD WILL BE A BETTER PLACE
IF MORE PEOPLE ARE ENGAGED AS VOLUNTEERS.

POINTS
OF LIGHT
FOUNDATION

Points of Light Foundation A non-profit organization dedicated to encouraging and facilitating volunteering, the Foundation expanded the function of its annual report to work as a promotional piece geared toward multiple audiences. The clean, sophisticated interior focuses on emotional photography and uses white space to maximal effect. This piece speaks to the heart and the mind.

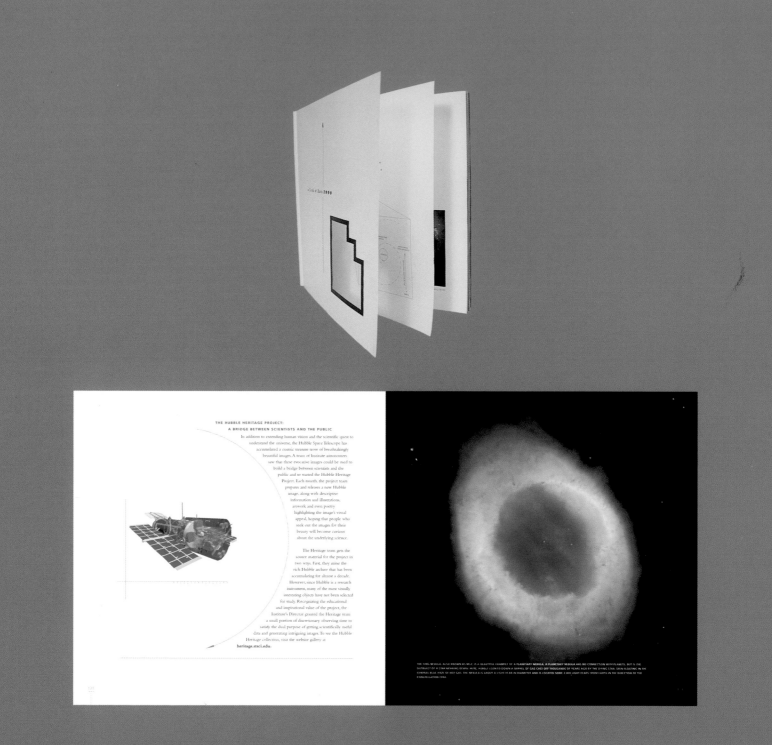

Association of University and Research Astronomers Both a marketing piece and a biennial report, this publication is unique in terms of its square format, die-cut cover and stunning photography. Refined typography and metallic-silver ink suggest the scientific precision that characterizes the association.

Benton Foundation The Benton Foundation works to realize the social benefits made possible through the public interest use of communications. The "What's Going On" series, published through its Communications Policy and Practice program, analyzes the interwoven roles of technology, philanthropy and community. The design of these two-color publications conveys the material with clarity and depth.

THAT'S ENTERTAINMENT

"Seen any good movies lately?"

"Seen any good movies lately?"

Chances are that since the top film at the box office on any given weekend can easily bring in 20 million dollars in ticket sales, a lot of people have seen a good movie or two. Perhaps that explains why the question has become as common a rhetorical refrain as "Nice day, isn't it?" or "What's new?"

Movies, television shows, sporting events, concerts, theater—society indulges in these activities in an effort to entertain itself. Whether after a tough day at work or during a long-awaited vacation, entertainment is a commodity that many consider necessary for survival. Unlike the essentials of food and shelter, however, entertainment is an intangible, ephemeral experience that occurs within a limited time frame.

A trip to the amusement park can last only as long as the park is open. These hours are savored with family or friends, until all that remains is to reminisce about the event with memories and pictures. Indeed, it is possible to keep a ticket stub, snap a picture or record a movie, but the experience cannot be replaced—unless it is experienced again.

It is this temporal quality of entertainment that makes it so... entertaining. The expectations for the two hours spent at a soccer game, or the week spent at the Olympics, are what drive most people to experience it in the first place.

While each event is transient and short-lived, the entertainment industry is large and well-established, and just as competitive as any other trade. This competition doesn't take place only on the field or at the box office. Society provides most people a limited number of hours each week with which to amuse themselves. Therefore, each form of entertainment fights for a highly limited attention span—and for an even more limited dollar.

In this environment, it is imperative that entertainment businesses develop images that clearly communicate the compelling diversions they have to offer. These images must do more than just convey their service as a commodity, however. They must capture the essence of the experience in a visual identity. Whether dynamic graphics, vibrant color or unique typography, the elements that form a perfectly packaged design strategy can hold the key to these companies' success.

IBM

As designer Paul Rand's horizontal blue bars had become immediately recognizable to consumers, it was only natural to combine them with images associated with the Olympic Games. As the blue stripes immediately and forcefully call IBM to mind, images such as the cauldron, rings and torch obviously suggest the world's most prestigious sporting event.

When Paul Rand created IBM's simple blue-striped logo in the 1950s, few expected that the concept would come to define the corporation's branding image as "Big Blue" into the 21st century. But it does. And IBM is one company with a keen appreciation of the power and influence behind design. • Founded in 1888 at the height of the Industrial Revolution, IBM grew from a tabulation and scale company based in New York City to a multinational corporation that defined workplace technology throughout the 20th century. From the launch of the first personal computer in 1981 to the ubiquity of today's e-business software, IBM has consistently represented the cutting edge of technological innovation and firmly established itself as a household name that is synonymous with success. • In 1956, Rand was hired as the graphic design consultant for

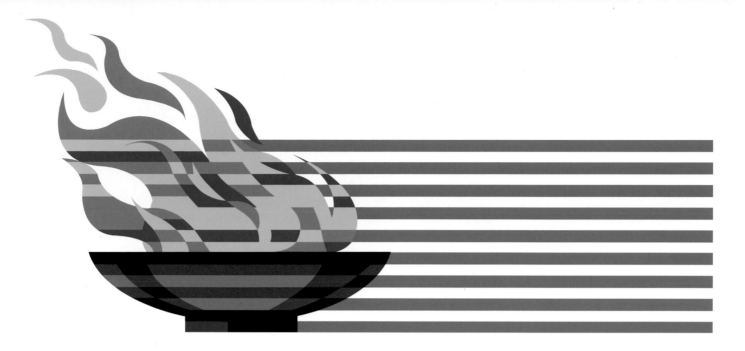

The design solution for IBM's corporate sponsorship identity integrates the distinctive blue stripes of the corporation's logo with graphics of traditional Olympic symbols and athletes in action.

IBM and created the corporation's logo and entire identity system. A pioneering American designer who relied on strong visual ideas and dynamic typography to convey a message, he applied modernist traditions in developing the simple, yet enduring logo. The logo was so enduring, in fact, that it was not until the 1996 Summer Olympic Games in Atlanta that IBM chose to debut a bold new approach to identity design and corporate sponsorship.

The centennial anniversary of the Modern Olympics, the 1996 Atlanta Games held fast to the traditions and practices that, decade after decade, had become familiar the world over. Building on such a universal influence, IBM analyzed its brand image and determined that its corporate sponsorship identity needed to communicate on a global scale. The design had to translate into hundreds of languages and relate to hundreds of cultures. In short, it had to convey the enormous appeal of the Olympics, and the well-known symbols and emotions that accompany it.

In each application of the design concept, simple but active illustrations feature vibrant color contrast that creates a sense of movement. Whether for postcards, mugs or billboards, the result is dynamic.

The strategy was twofold: Promote both IBM's sponsorship of the Games, and the Olympics themselves. In doing so, reinvent the corporation's image, creating a concept that augments its already strong and effective branding approach. Accordingly, the solution integrates the distinctive blue stripes of IBM's existing logo with graphics of traditional Olympic symbols and athletes in action.

As Rand's horizontal blue bars had become immediately recognizable to consumers, it was only natural to combine them with images associated with the Games. As the blue stripes immediately and forcefully call IBM to mind, images such as the cauldron, rings and torch obviously suggest the world's most prestigious sporting event. Forming a highly effective visual message, the blue stripes are incorporated into the design and IBM is reflected as an integral part of the Olympics—ensuring that the two elements are inseparably blended. Most importantly, they are melded seamlessly, allowing the viewer to focus on IBM's broad participation in the event, rather than the corporation's products.

From the historic torch relay to the philosophy, *"Citius, altius, fortius,"* these traditions are richly illustrated with a design approach that is distinctively global. In all, 30 different illustrations of sports icons are layered among IBM's blue bars. A colorful spectrum of athletes including gymnasts,

IBM has be...
Olympic Games since
providing a growing level of
information processing support.
In 1993, IBM signed a long term
agreement with the International
Olympic Committee as the
Worldwide Information Technology
Sponsor through the year 2000.

IBM
Worldwide Information
Technology Sponsor

IBM
Worldwide Information
Technology Sponsor

Atlant...

IBM
Worldwide Information
Technology · Sponsor

equestrians, swimmers and cyclists, as well as a flaming Olympic torch and a triumphant medal winner, complete the sponsorship identity.

In each design, simple but active illustrations are rendered more striking by dynamic color contrast and juxtaposed white space, leaving no question as to the focal point of the piece. Vibrant tones of yellow, red, green and purple create a sense of movement, which is emphasized by the portions of the illustrations that just escape the boundaries of the blue stripes.

IBM's "Look of the Games" was applied to dozens of promotional vehicles, from mouse pads, lapel pins, hats, T-shirts, jackets and posters, to billboards, buses and truck sides.

Incorporating the equity of the blue bars with the immediately identifiable Olympic symbols, the design is at once distinct and inclusive. It brings varied cultures and distant people together while setting the corporation apart from all other sponsors.

Few initiatives have as positive an impact on a company's image as Olympic sponsorship. Similarly, few design concepts are so enduring as IBM's. Their well-conceived message was communicated through a number of promotional avenues, emphasized by an engaging and appropriate look that balances graphic innovation and marketing strategy.

Confident in the branding elements introduced in 1996, IBM adopted the same design approach for its sponsorship of the 1998 Winter Games in Nagano and the 2000 Summer Games in Sydney. The new Olympics-inspired design concept was also applied throughout the company, affecting branding and advertising on a grand scale and fostering a renewed spirit of pride in the staff.

IBM's "Look of the Games" features dozens of athletes and symbols from the Olympic Games and is applied to a number of promotional materials. These include printed materials, mouse pads and canvas bags.

Discovery Communications, Inc. This series of graphic icons promotes some of The Discovery Channel's educational programs. A clever combination of title and descriptive illustration gives a quick idea of program content. The icons were used on printed materials and also manufactured into rubber stamps, allowing the company to customize bags and accessories without expense.

Professional Golfers Association The biggest challenge posed by PGA Tour's annual report was to include photos of the Tour's players without making each page look like the rest. The solution was contained in the use of color boxes, rules and geometric graphic elements, adding depth and texture to each page and section.

Wana Zoo Careful contrast makes the identity system for Asia's Wana Zoo effective. Colorful animal drawings communicate with children, while black backgrounds add sophistication that suggests the zoo is fun for adults. Juxtaposing a classical typeface with playful, hieroglyphic animals emphasizes this concept. Since no two visits to the zoo are alike, the logo can feature a handful of different animals.

ADDRESS BOOK

WANA ZOO

NAVA NAVA's promotions capture the long-gone elegance of cruising the open seas. Today, the luxury cruise line offers excursions down such exotic waterways as Thailand's Chao Phraya and India's Ganges. Posters, dinnerware and amenities are reminiscent of a time when traveling was a destination in itself.

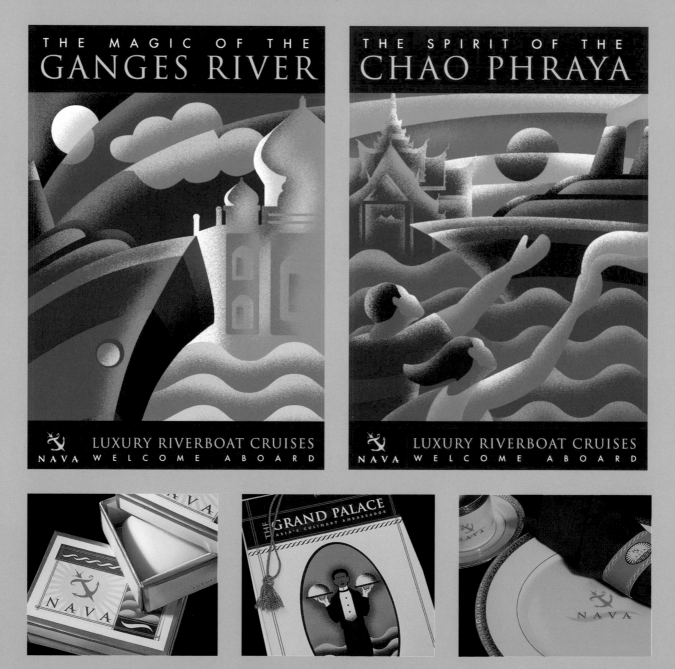

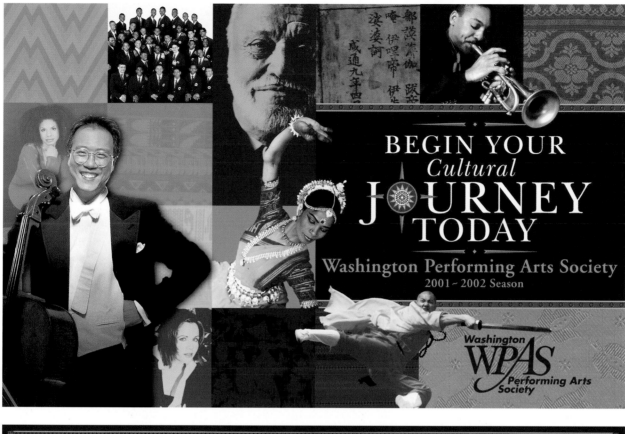

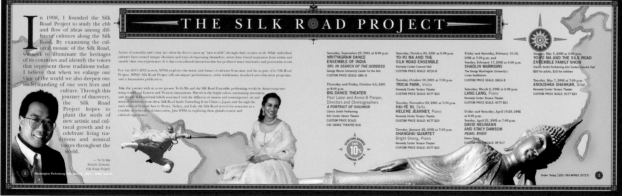

Washington Performing Arts Society The design of this subscription brochure promoting a series of Asian-related cultural performances built on the identity originated in an earlier WPAS season brochure. The imagery and content for this piece, however, is purely East meets West, inspired by the effort's exotic title, "The Silk Road Project."

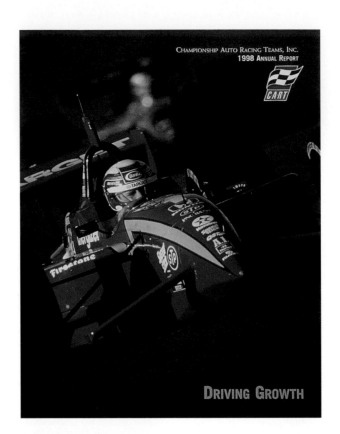

Championship Auto Racing Teams The design strategy behind CART's annual report was to highlight the aspect of the organization that matters most—the drivers. Dramatic action photos of CART's winningest racers appear every few pages. Just like in racing, sponsors are also given prominence, adding pleasing dashes of color to a report that is clean and clear throughout.

Wearhouse The recycled paper and nuances of color used in this labeling system suggest the natural quality of the upscale line of athletic socks. Various sports, including weightlifting and track and field, are depicted in a series of illustrations. Horizontal lines convey high energy.

U.S. Open Cool, sophisticated graphics were selected for T-shirts on sale at the U.S. Open. Designs focus on several themes, including New York City, the international aspect of the tournament and the game of tennis itself. Semi-abstract, hand-drawn, humorous and urban approaches create a range of designs that appeal to the event's diverse enthusiasts.

NYC 2012 This illustration, used on a T-shirt and other give-away items, promotes the Big Apple's efforts to be named host city for the Summer Olympic Games of 2012. Imagery of a universally recognized landmark—the Statue of Liberty—is used in creative, unexpected ways to portray America's largest metropolis as the choice for best venue.

OPPOSITE: Black Entertainment Television BET sought to solidify its presence by expanding its affiliate base. These marketing materials promote the breadth and diversity of BET's several networks. Brightly colored brochures for each network function both on their own and when assembled into an overall sales kit.

The Coca-Cola Company Consulting efforts related to Coca-Cola's sponsorship of the 1996 Atlanta Olympic Games resulted in a vast array of recommended designs and applications. Among these were T-shirts, posters, billboards, truck panels, shopping bags and sports bottles. Several full campaigns were designed, each targeting a specific market niche.

Wolf Trap This outdoor performing arts center is known for hosting exceptional music, dance and theater events. Its summer promotional campaign required a hand-drawn design that could be used on T-shirts, brochures, posters and buses. Hues emphasize warm weather; the outdoor theme conveys community.

LEFT TO RIGHT: **Space Adventures, space-related travel and recreation company; Cow Parade, international art exhibition; U.S. Tennis Association, Arthur Ashe Kids' Day event; International Gay and Lesbian Football Association, soccer association; ISL Marketing, under-17 youth soccer tournament; The first Tee, PGA program devised to promote the sport of golfing.**

A SIGN OF THE TIMES

From the Egyptian sun dial to the locomotive,
each heralds steps in the march of progress.

About 5,000 years ago, Neolithic people in what is now known as Mesopotamia settled in fertile plains and developed the wheel, the sailboat and tools made of copper and bronze.

Last year, scientists decoded the 33.5 million pieces of a human chromosome, beginning the sequence of billions of chemicals that compose DNA and determine each person's characteristics, from eye color to intelligence.

Technology has changed the world and changed lives in ways that are almost beyond comprehension. Whether incremental advances or an unexpected discovery that brings a watershed of change, technological innovation seems a guaranteed constant.

Just as people have learned to embrace technology and apply it to the improvement of everyday life, businesses have harnessed technology and adapted it to a commercial level. The explosion of "dot com" companies, conducting business through the ubiquitous Internet, is the most obvious—and talked about—example of this transformation. A single home page is now a customer's real-time link to products, services and interactive communi-

cation. Companies are using this global network to market their products and themselves.

But not all of today's advances lie in the use of the Internet as the newest medium. Businesses are also finding that technology is a hot commodity, just as the telephone and motorized car once were. From cutting-edge computer software to global digital broadcasting, companies are providing access to the technology that simplifies and enhances our lives.

It seems more difficult to encapsulate technology as a concept or science than as a movement. The Egyptian sun dial, printing press, cotton gin and locomotive each herald steps in the endless march of progress. As the march goes on, businesses will continue to make the most of these discoveries and their application to our lives.

Businesses will also demand design and marketing concepts that clearly communicate their comprehension of these advancements. The following companies have succeeded on all counts, with strong and compelling graphic marketing materials that highlight the possibilities that technology brings.

MUSEUM OF COLLECTIBLE ARTIFACTS ONLINE

Inspired by one man's passion for collecting, the Museum of Collectible Artifacts was launched in 1999 as a resource for serious collectors and casual hobbyists alike. Realizing the Internet's potential as a vehicle to unite those who enjoy collecting, he created an online forum where these groups could come together.

It is said that one man's trash is another's treasure. Whether there is a classic head vase in the attic collecting dust, or an old lunch box in the garage organizing nuts and bolts, everyone has a kitschy item from the past that just never goes away. Perhaps it should have been discarded long ago. Chances are that it features a now defunct rock group or a discontinued television sit-com, or captures the style and spirit of an era gone by. • Why is this cultural relic so difficult to throw away? For one, it just might be worth something. Yet even if it isn't worth a dime, it tugs on the heart strings and represents a memory of a different time and place, when life was simpler, days were longer and a smile could change the world. • This

is the premise behind the Museum of Collectible Artifacts Online. Featuring everything from retro posters to vintage wind-up toys, and from whimsical cookie jars to nostalgic lunch boxes, MOCA is a community-based online museum filled with exhibits of collectible treasures from around the world.

Inspired by one man's passion for collecting, MOCA was launched in 1999 as a resource for serious collectors and casual hobbyists alike. Realizing the Internet's potential as a vehicle to unite those who enjoy collecting, he created an online forum where these groups could come together. Unlike other sites that focus on one type of collectible item—like lunch boxes or miniature stuffed animals—or function as portals that direct

collectors to outside resources, MOCA is a destination in itself.

A practical, educational and inspirational tool, the website offers colorful images, historical backgrounds and reliable pricing information for every one of the various artifacts in the gallery. Perhaps most importantly, though, the Museum is a hub of activity.

Users can pose questions about their treasures, post information about upcoming expositions and exhibits and share their collections directly on the site. Silent auctions allow collectors to bid on a variety of exclusive items, while bulletin boards function as classified advertisements for merchandise that can be bought and sold. A collector can

A promotional brochure targeted to potential sponsors of the website details the distinct benefits of advertising with MOCA Online. The site's far-reaching appeal and community-based approach are presented in a compelling visual display.

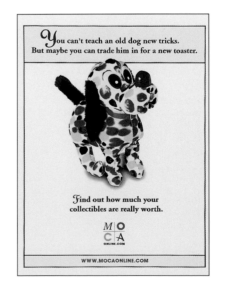

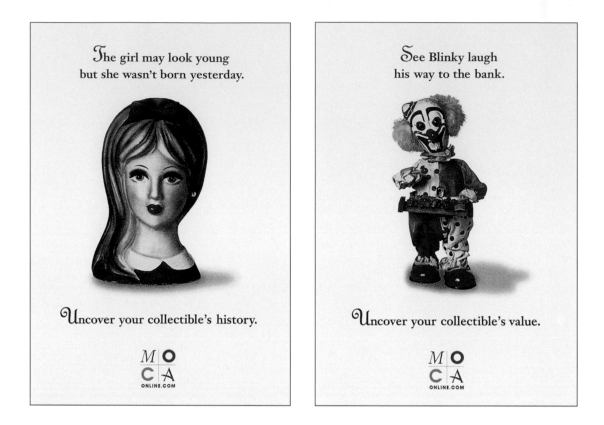

The girl may look young
but she wasn't born yesterday.

Uncover your collectible's history.

See Blinky laugh
his way to the bank.

Uncover your collectible's value.

MOCA's advertising campaign generates a great deal of exposure for the Museum. The straightforward, yet humorous approach and the colorful memorabilia resonate with collectors of all interests and capture MOCA Online's community spirit.

find out how much money a kung fu lunch box might fetch in the marketplace, and then track down someone interested in purchasing it.

As sales of newly trendy items like beanbags, music boxes and die-cast toys have accelerated in recent years, MOCA has become an oasis for these popular products as well. This mingling of old and new, established and novel, antique and modern, is a key element of the website's attraction.

In determining the architecture of the site, simple navigation and straightforward language were of

paramount concern. The primary objective was to encourage a community atmosphere that attracts a broad base of visitors—and their diverse collecting interests.

MOCA also had to implement a design concept that would allow the intriguing, friendly and often comical images of the collectibles to stand out. Colors remain muted overall, as cymbal-crashing monkeys and drum-playing bears bring each page to life. Typography mixes upper and lower cases and italic and bold faces, emphasizing the site's assorted content.

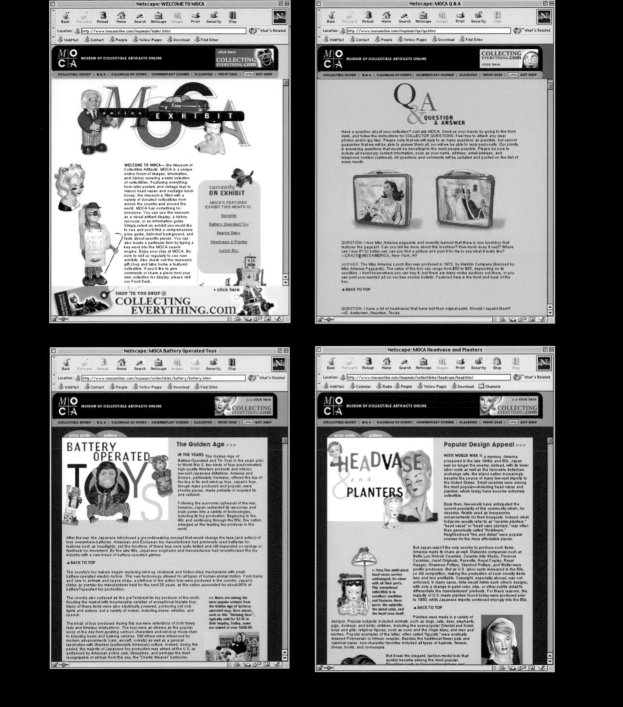

Virtual exhibits on the MOCA website allow collectors to retrieve information, display their collections and browse for new additions. Its easy, spirited and informative attitude is reflected throughout every page.

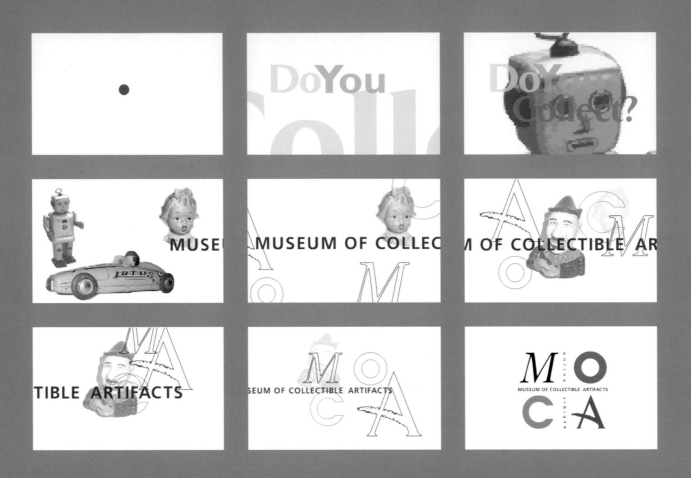

A flash page was developed as a dramatic and memorable entrance to the MOCA website. Although consistent with the overall identity of the online museum, the flash features kinetic typography and imagery that rightly heightens expectations for the site.

Key elements from the MOCA website design extend to letterhead, envelopes and business cards. Bright colors and imaginative placement suggest MOCA's fun environment, while the presence of cute collectibles brings a smile to the reader's face.

Featured exhibits are indicated with large graphic icons that represent each collection. Mousing over the monkey results in a cymbal-crash; the beautiful lady head vase gives a wink. Clicking on the icon leads to a short but informative introduction of the exhibit's history. (It is discovered, for example, that head vases were originally used by florists as inexpensive planters and enhancements for bouquets.) The user is then directed to either a gallery of selected collectibles or a pricing guide that estimates the value of items in fair, good and excellent condition.

Key elements of the website are extended to collateral materials and print advertisements. The simple, clean MOCA Online logo—integrating the varied typographic treatments used throughout the site—is given an unconventional position on stationery and envelopes. Completing the

look, one of several collectibles is tucked sweetly into a lower corner.

Advertisements direct collectors to the website with witty copy and prominent placement of some of the most universally appealing collectors' items. Driving the site's utility as a resource for determining a product's value and history, the ads speak directly to their primary audiences—those who are serious about collecting or fascinated by the pastime.

Collecting is an activity that unites men and women, teenagers and seniors, and lawyers and artists. Motivated by a common love of treasures from the past, collectors have discovered a fun, simple way to capture a special moment, or inspire a nostalgic vision. The Museum of Collectible Artifacts allows them to share in the joy together.

Intelligent Transport Society of America/National Trade Productions
The logo for the 9th World Congress, sponsored in part by ITS America, incorporates the 2002 event's Chicago location with the Congress's globe—in which a stylized "A" suggests a highway, flight path or more abstract objective. Marketing materials feature imagery of Windy City landmarks with striped bands to suggest technology.

LEFT TO RIGHT: AdviceZone.com, personal and professional advice website; AdJuggler, Internet advertisement management program; Varsitybooks.com, online resource for university books; Gunnison, Internet support company; AOL Foundation, program using the media for the public's interest; CycleShark.com, online motorcycle parts and accessories retailer.

TeleBright.com An entire marketing identity was needed for TeleBright.com, an unbiased resource for small- to medium-sized businesses to peruse, compare and purchase telecommunications services. The concept of this "bright idea" is portrayed by a light bulb, but in a way that doesn't appear trite. Applications include stationery, pocket folders, advertisements and website.

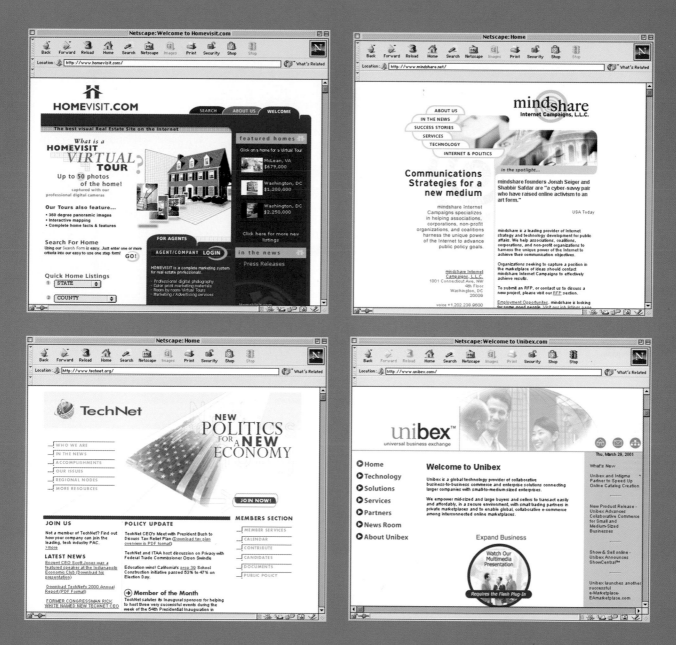

LEFT TO RIGHT: HomeVisit, online real estate resource; mindshare, Internet strategy and technology development firm; TechNet, technology policy advocacy organization; Universal Business Exchange, business-to-business electronic commerce facilitator.

Iridium Iridium's satellite-based telephony allows subscribers to communicate with anyone in the world. The company's annual report emphasizes its global reach by superimposing its "big dipper" logo on scenes from around the world. Clean, light, but striking graphics suggest freedom, ease and communications.

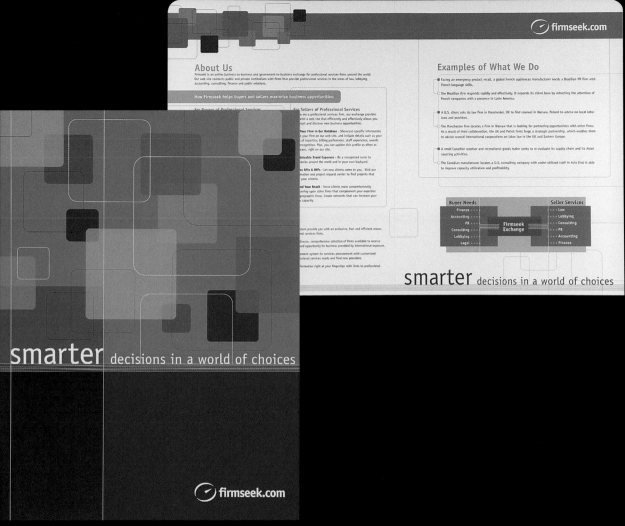

Firmseek Whether public relations, lobbying or legal, Firmseek connects businesses with firms that offer professional services worldwide. The pleasing layout of its brochures offers a perfect solution for the information-rich company. Basic colors and geometric shapes emphasize a structured, organized design, similar to the company's business approach.

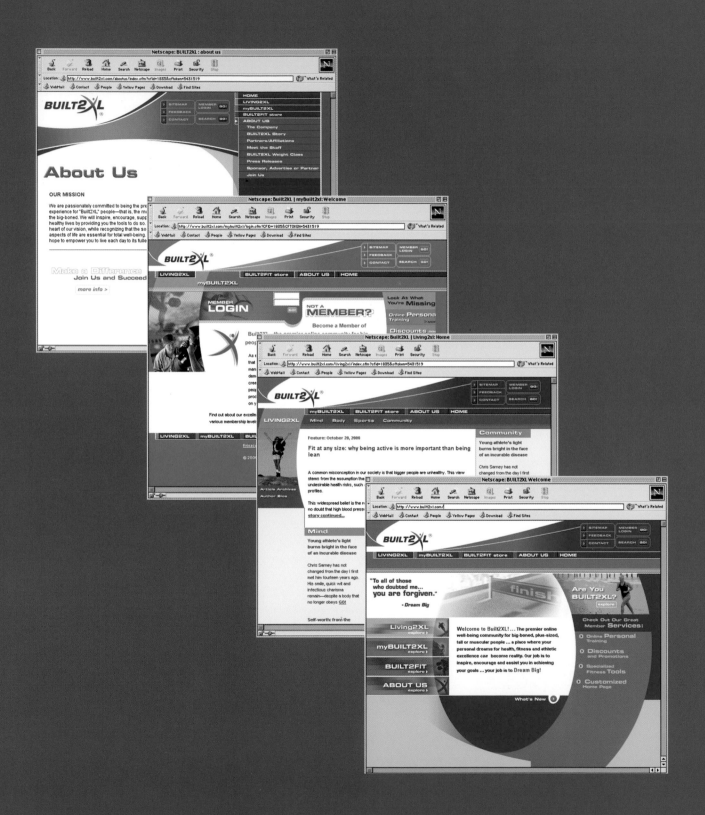

Built2XL An online well-being community for big-boned, tall and plus-sized people, Built2XL is committed to total fitness and vitality. Its logo focuses on an outstretched "X" that represents the human form at its most exultant. Its movement conveys strength and vigor and reflects an attitude that encourages fitness inside and out. The website and print materials feature an energetic design that celebrates life.

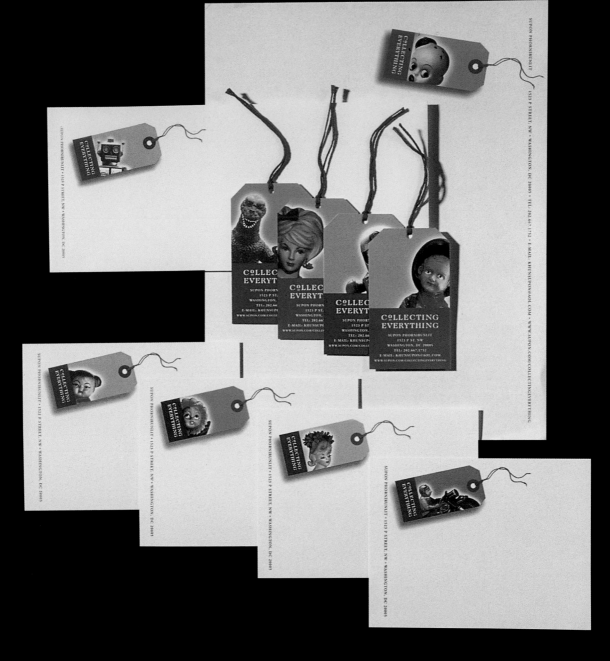

Collecting Everything Collateral materials for a website that sells antique and hard-to-find collectibles are as fun as the site itself. The business card is actually a hang tag—complete with string—that features one of a number of nostalgic characters. The letterhead adapts the look, but retains the fun.

AllowanceNet The leading online allowance management system for kids and their parents, AllowanceNet helps children take responsibility for their chores and gives them confidence in earning, spending and managing money. The design is fun and colorful—appealing to children while conveying reliability and security to adults.

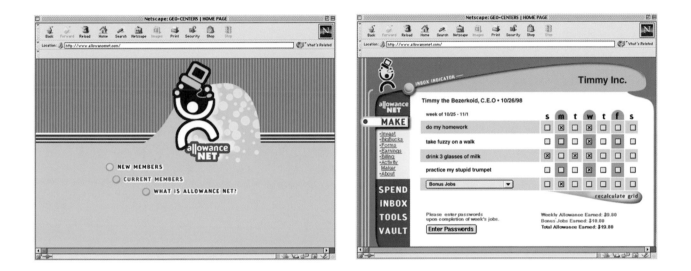

TeleworX

DATACAST

LEFT TO RIGHT: SignedBy.com, auction website; TeleworX, technical consulting and engineering firm; Velao, electronic mortgage industry services company; Datacast, digital broadcasting and transmission services firm; ServerVault, Internet security services company; Thruport Technologies, browser-based applications company.

Step9 Software An engaging flash animation effectively integrates this company's varied services with its logo. Like on its print marketing materials, strong green bars stand out, but only so much as to draw the eye to the logo, effectively branding the corporation for its customers.

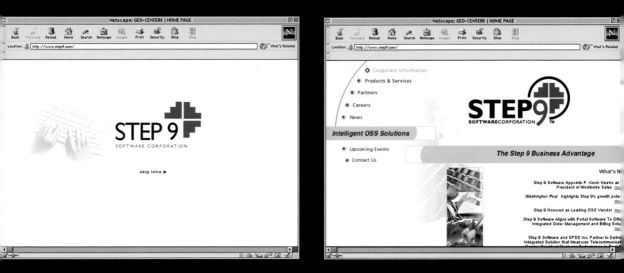

GEO-CENTERS This research company works with laboratories and institutions to find scientific solutions to the challenges of today—and tomorrow. Its website is intended to recruit employees. A people-oriented design focuses on the company's inventive atmosphere, while the logo reflects its progressive philosophy.

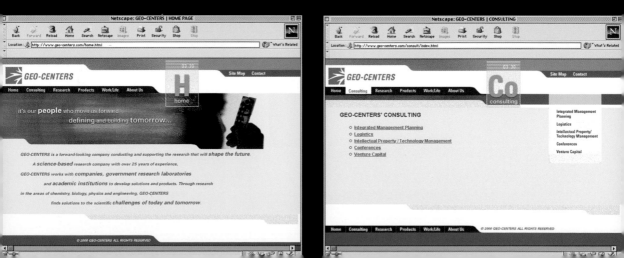

Cvent.com Facilitating event planning for meeting professionals and marketers, Cvent.com boasts a flexible collection of online invitations that saves time and effort, encourages quick responses and can be customized with a company's text and logo.

America Online **AOL sponsored an online effort with HelpingHands.org to encourage charitable giving during the holidays. A dozen celebrities created original, signed artwork related to the "helping hands" theme, which were then auctioned on the Internet to raise money for charity. A poster commemorates the program's kick-off. The identity was also applied to a DVD case and insert.**

TeleworX A bold red "X" and a bright yellow "O" form the foundation for this software and engineering consulting firm, whose products all begin or end with "X." The overall look suggests dynamism and differentiates the TeleworX marketing identity from that of its competitors.

SCHOOLS OF THOUGHT

It's more than sonnets and economics.

It is said that those who do not learn from history are doomed to repeat it. What about Calculus? French? Wood shop?

From the first day of kindergarten to college convocation and beyond, education fills the mind. Whether it is invited with wide-open arms or fought bitterly every step of the way, there is no doubt that learning broadens a person's horizons and motivates thought and inquiry.

Nowhere is this more true than in the halls of colleges and universities around the country. It is in these microcosmic environments that education often becomes appreciated—as more than reading, 'riting and 'rithmetic—as an investment. Institutions of higher learning, whether broad, liberal arts-based colleges or specialty technical schools, all provide students with foundations for life in the outside world.

At elementary and graduate schools as well, education teaches more than sonnets and economics. It encourages research, investigation and community service, it provides skills for social well-being, and it gives a preview of the working world. In essence, education throws open doors that previously may have been locked. The changing face of technology enhances all of this, increasing access and understanding in ways never thought possible.

But schools now face an interesting challenge. Most parents are already convinced that a good education is a sound investment. The percentage of students attending and completing college—and beyond—is skyrocketing. Rather, the challenge is to stand out from a crowd. Each institution must now demonstrate why its offerings are superior.

Whether via print materials or websites, schools must tap into what drives prospective students in their search for the perfect educational experience. With fresh and dynamic design, previously lackluster recruitment materials and confusing messages become sparkling, creative and—most importantly—inviting new identities.

The examples that follow illustrate successful transformations that not only boosted images, but admissions rates as well. These educational centers have borrowed some creativity and imagination from the classroom and put it to work in design.

THE
GEORGE WASHINGTON
UNIVERSITY

The strategy for The George Washington University's new recruitment materials was clear: Emphasize the school's urban environment, academic quality and international scope, and appeal to college-bound, visually-oriented youth while holding the interest of their parents.

President George Washington had long encouraged the establishment of a national university in Washington, D.C. It was his hope that such an institution would provide eager students an opportunity to learn the arts and sciences while gaining firsthand knowledge of the theories of good citizenship and republican government. In 1821, his hope was realized by a group of ministers and laymen and approved by President Monroe. • In the 21st century, encouraging prospective students to attend a particular university is a more challenging and complicated task. Recruitment materials for high-profile educational institutions must not just exist, but stand out in the increasingly sophisticated and competitive marketplace of college admissions. • The George Washington University

something
happens
here

something
happens
here

something
happens
here

CAMPUS

THE GEORGE WASHINGTON UNIVERSITY
WASHINGTON, DC

how you should use the classroom brochure

"Something Happens Here: Classroom" exclusively highlights the GW classroom experience.
We think that what happens in our classrooms is distinctive enough to merit its own publication.
Read it in combination with our other publications:

"something happens here: campus"

"something happens here: city"

▶ the advantages and opportunities of each part of the GW experience.

▶ they come together as you prioritize or reset your college goals and interests.

▶ as, ambitions, and talents to GW and hit the ground running. Are you ready?

something
happens
here

THE GEORGE WASHINGTON UNIVERSITY

come to class ▶▶

participate in our intellectual life

Our academic tradition and vitality is summarily the "quest for understanding." What happens in the classroom captures the essence and value of a GW education: an enthusiastic commitment to research, exploration, creativity, and integrity on a very personal level. There are few private schools of our size with 7,000 undergraduates that have the number of majors and array of classroom experiences. You will be inspired by the kinds of individualized academic interests and pursuits that GW students undertake. You will be amazed by the volume of academic resources & privileged access available to our students in the classroom, on campus, and in the city. Our professors are engaging, eminently qualified, and well-connected. In combination, these factors create a robust intellectual community of students, faculty, opportunities, opinions, and ideas.

faced just such a hurdle in 1992, suffering from a decline in the number and the quality of student applications received. In the extremely competitive environment within which top universities work, GW was struggling to recruit the handful of students desired by all schools. It needed to reverse the trend.

After a thorough collection and examination of all current marketing materials used by GW—and even those of competing schools—what was immediately evident was difficult for the University's senior staff to accept: The materials were conservative, dated and too greatly focused on academics. Lackluster admissions were largely

due to the traditional look and feel of existing recruitment pieces, which featured navy backgrounds, gold type and white Capitol buildings—not at all compelling for high school students used to bold, flashy, quickly changing graphics and music videos. The institution had to revive its publications with a whole new campaign.

To that end, the strategy for GW's new recruitment materials was clear: Emphasize the school's urban environment, academic quality and international scope, and appeal to college-bound, visually-oriented youth while holding the interest of their parents. In short, GW would recreate the feelings and images associated with

A series of three brochures focusing on campus, classroom and city replaces the single-piece viewbook originally designed for GW. The new format communicates the excitement of living and learning in Washington, D.C. to the 15-to 17-year-old MTV generation.

Fun cookie jars based on the GW trolley are among the items given to high school students who visit the campus before selecting a college.

living smack in the middle of downtown Washington, D.C.—the most recognized city in the world—and all the excitement and opportunities that accompany it. The approach held more promise than academic-looking catalogs with pictures of the capital's landmarks.

After reaching a clear understanding of the institution's marketing objectives, it was time to focus on the audience: 15-to 17-year-old prospective undergraduates. The challenge was to tap into what drives these students and develop a

system of visual solutions that would appeal to their sensibilities, capturing the University's dynamic offerings in order to attract a greater number of qualified undergraduates.

The design solution balances bright and exciting colors with generous but accessible text, emphasizing the University's academic excellence, quality of life and significant Washington, D.C., location. The energetic images appeal to a young audience at the same time that manageable information engages parents and high school counselors.

New recruitment materials are a dramatic change from the scholarly, navy blue-and-gold pieces GW previously had used to communicate with college-bound high school students.

THE GEORGE WASHINGTON UNIVERSITY
WASHINGTON, DC

international
students and
u.s. students
living abroad

something
happens
here

thing
appens
e

CAMPUS

The George Washington University

The George Washington University
WASHINGTON DC

The University's recruitment website was modernized to complement its new print materials, effectively incorporating cutting-edge technology and dynamic graphics to create an energetic online experience.

A hip and fun multimedia film completes the high-tech look and feel of GW's engaging website—an appropriate resource for high school students used to flashy graphics and videos.

Various promotions are sent to high school sophomores, juniors and seniors, all of whom are poised to make important decisions concerning their futures. In each viewbook and brochure, bold photos and graphics wow the reader, minimalist covers contrast with active interior spreads, headlines compete for attention, and the aggressive, oversized format doesn't hold back. Themes such as "Something Happens Here" and "You will..." raise expectations high—then deliver.

The design not only carries GW's messages successfully, but visually conveys the University's broad attractions and possibilities to its target audience of prospective students. GW's recruitment website was also modernized to complement the new printed materials, incorporating cutting-edge technology and dynamic enhancements that reflect online trends and demonstrate the institution's exciting environment.

Designed to encourage GW students to live on campus in residence halls, two distinctive posters promote the networking services available through the University's dormitories, which are all equipped with high-speed Internet connections.

In 1992, The George Washington University's new recruiting campaign garnered impressive—and immediate—results. Since that initial redesign, GW has updated the look and feel of its recruitment materials every two years, enjoying a dramatic increase in admissions with each new series.

Most recently, a very high-tech, almost corporate approach emphasizes the University's recent investment in technology. A series of three different brochures—campus, classroom and city—replace the previous single-piece viewbook format. The brochures feature metallic—almost futuristic—colors, silver mylar carrier envelopes, and corresponding DVDs, CD-ROMs and website to complement GW's new foray into high-tech recruiting. Direct mail postcards and other publications follow the initial items in order to maximize response. These materials, too, contribute to a current jump in admissions rates.

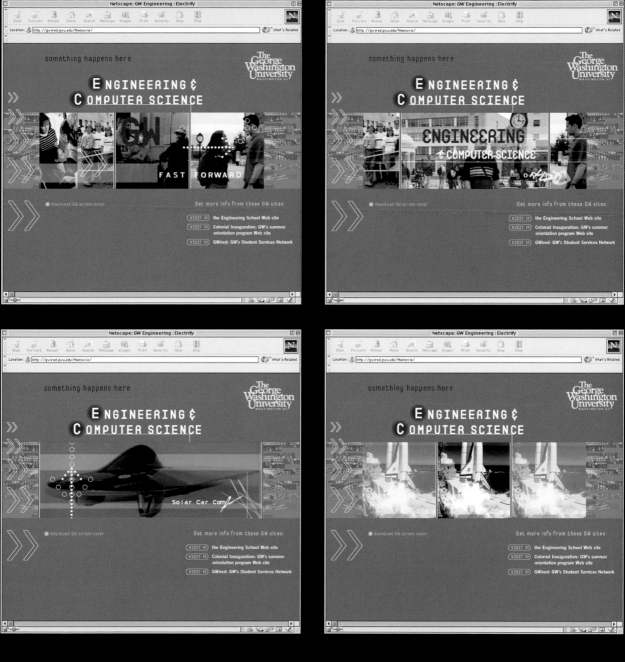

The Engineering School adopts an online presence that incorporates many characteristics of the recruitment website. An electrifying film introduces the experiences—from solar cars to flight simulation—that await engineering and computer science students.

Episcopal High School Episcopal is a preparatory institution that stresses individual excellence, dynamic academics and a strong residential community spirit. Inviting design and compelling campus photography—both in print and online admissions materials—capture these qualities.

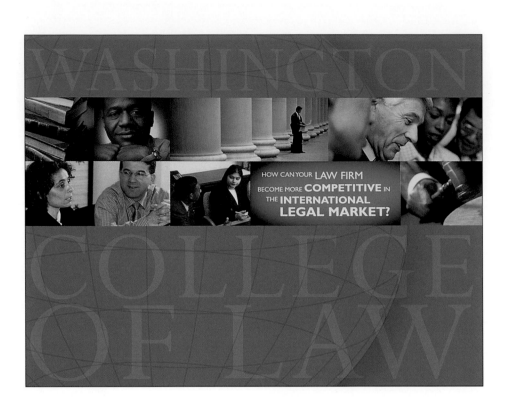

American University, Washington College of Law **The law school's marketing identity is modern, clean and professional. Print pieces vary depending on the market niche or purpose. The intellectual property direct mailer, for instance, targets law firms recruiting new WCL graduates. Its message is quick, to the point and current.**

The Practice of IP Law
is no longer limited to Copyright, Patent & Trademark
Why should the Teaching of IP Law
be any Different ?

AMERICAN UNIVERSITY
WASHINGTON COLLEGE OF LAW
OFFICE OF CAREER SERVICES
4801 MASSACHUSETTS AVENUE, NW, STE 515
WASHINGTON, DC 20016-8186

FIRST-CLASS MAIL
U.S. POSTAGE
PAID
PERMIT NO. 1158
WASHINGTON, D.C.

INNOVATIVE COURSES

Courses in New Technology

E-COMMERCE LAW & DRAFTING Focuses on the practical legal and drafting issues facing licensors, licensees and developers and users of computer software, hardware, multimedia works and on-line information.

LAW OF ELECTRONIC PRIVACY Explores how courts and Congress seek to protect information privacy as new technologies and new institutional practices emerge.

LAW IN CYBERSPACE Reviews the application of current laws to the Internet and proposals for new or revised laws to regulate the developing Global Information Infrastructure.

LAW IN THE INFORMATION SOCIETY Examines the treatment of information by law and lays out the main legal, economic and political models for the ownership and control of information.

INTERNATIONAL CONTRACTS & THE TRANSFER OF IP RIGHTS Examines international contracts and litigation; Patent, Trademark and Copyright transactions; and the negotiation of license agreements.

Core IP Courses

U.S. Trademark Law
Advanced Copyright
Entertainment Law
Intellectual Property Law
International & Comparative Copyright Law
International & Professional Sports
Law of Professional Sports
Law & the Visual Arts
Media Law
Patent Law
International & Comparative Trademark Law

Specialized Business & Technology Courses

The Law of Venture Capital
Business Planning
Advanced Corporate Law
International Business Taxation
Federal Corporate Income Tax
Unfair Trade Practices & Consumer Protection
Advanced Antitrust
Mergers & Acquisitions
Telecommunications Law
Securities Regulation
Lawyer Bargaining
International Business Transactions

LLM in IP & Information Policy

A unique opportunity through the Law & Government Program to focus on the regulatory and policy aspects of IP law and technology.

WHAT are my HOUSING choices?
WHERE am I going to LIVE?

Housing

AT ALA, WE KNOW THAT HOUSING ISN'T A LITTLE IMPORTANT, IT'S VERY IMPORTANT!

At ALA, we think housing is so important that every ALA location has a Director of Housing. He or she will work with you to make sure that where you live is right and comfortable for you. Did you tell us you wanted a homestay and now you want to live on campus? That's okay. The Director of Housing will be happy to arrange new housing for you. The application in the back of this catalog has a special section on housing. Fill it out with as many details as possible and send it to us right away. We'll send you information about your housing placement as soon as possible. You'll know exactly where you'll live before you even get on the plane.

> I've been with my host family for eight months. I have a great time during my stay. Every day we speak and talk a lot. On the weekends we usually go to the movies, basketball games, or a coffee shop. The food is the thing that I like most about my host family. My host father cooks the dinner and prepares the breakfast. He is a great cook. We have a great place for watching TV. They have a fridge and microwave for the students. The family has four kids. All of them are funny and friendly with me. Therefore, I'd like to stay with them more, but I need to go to college. They taught me a lot of stuff.

SELAHATTIN CEM ARAS,
Student at ALA/Boston Downtown
Gaziantep, Turkey

My stay in the dormitory was a terrific experience because I had the opportunity to live with an American girl and a Brazilian girl. We spent a lot of time speaking and practicing our English. I learned many things I never had before like how to do the laundry and to cook. It was amazing. Sometimes we invited some friends to the dorm and made a little party. We cooked and gossiped and so many things. It was amazing and I never would change that experience for anything in the world.

SHEILA MEMBREÑO,
Student at ALA/Merrimack College
Panama City, Panama

We all thoroughly enjoy serving as a host family. Our two children, Dara, 14 years old, and Brent, 12 years old, especially love it. They love to ask the students questions about their countries. They enjoy telling the students about America and comparing the two. We all look forward to getting to know each student and their unique personalities. Most of the students are easy to please and seem to enjoy and appreciate anything we may offer. We have taught two of our students to drive a car, and they each got their driver's licenses and bought a car! Overall, it is a wonderful experience for the whole family. Even our dog Sweetness enjoys all the extra attention!

DEBBIE ALTMAN,
Host Mother at ALA/The University of Tampa

Students who attend American Language Academy are a welcome addition to the student community at Butler University. Students from the University have the opportunity to interact and learn from each other... these interactions enhance every student's experience...

BETH A...
Direct...

12

American Language Academy

LEARN
English
IN the
USA

ENGLISH LANGUAGE PROGRAMS

BOSTON NEW YORK CITY SAN FRANCISCO CLEVELAND
PHILADELPHIA INDIANAPOLIS NORTH ANDOVER ASHLAND
STOCKTON PORTLAND PUEBLO TAMPA LAKE FOREST POUGHKEEPSIE

LEARN
English
IN the
USA

BOSTON NEW YORK CITY SAN FRANCISCO CLEVELAND
PHILADELPHIA INDIANAPOLIS NORTH ANDOVER ASHLAND
STOCKTON PORTLAND PUEBLO TAMPA LAKE FOREST POUGHKEEPSIE

ENGLISH LANGUAGE PROGRAMS

American Language Academy ALA offers programs that encourage international students to come to America, improve their English and experience the life of a typical U.S. student. Each promotional brochure targets a specific audience and demonstrates the breadth of cultural, academic and social experiences awaiting them. Materials are translated into a variety of European and Asian languages.

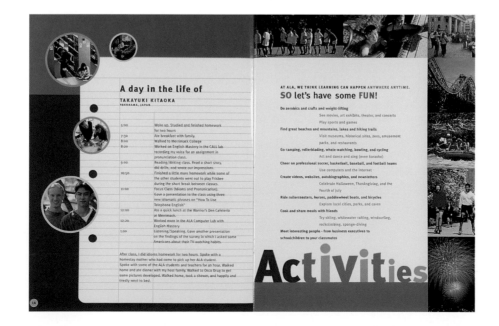

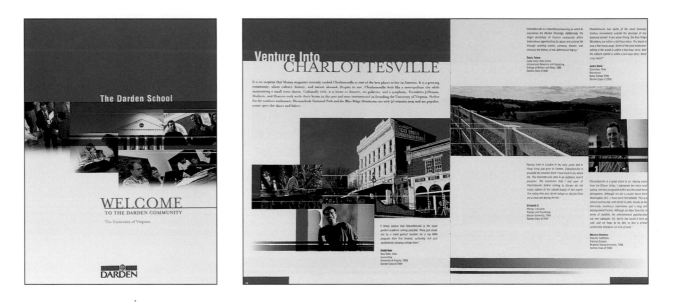

Darden School of Business Darden is the graduate school of business at the University of Virginia. As competition to recruit qualified students increases every year, the objective for this viewbook was to stand out from other schools' materials. A bright orange cover and bold title—Changing the Way You Think—do exactly that. An online version of the viewbook continues the visual identity with a clean, easy-to-follow interface.

DARDEN MBA PR

DARDEN MBA APPLICATION 2000

CREATING A NEW VISION

"I contemplate the University of Virginia as the future bulwark of the human mind in this hemisphere."
—Thomas Jefferson, 1820

STRETCH + SUPPORT →
PROFESSIONAL DEVELOPMENT

Darden has a distinctive point of view about management education. We believe our MBA program is the world's best because of our faculty's unwavering commitment to both the educational and professional development of our students.

We attract and develop people who want to lead, own, create and transform substantial business enterprises. Darden has an unmatched ability to integrate the functional areas of business, and to nail them firmly to the realities of a global, high-tech marketplace where the scarce resource will be leaders who can combine expertise, wisdom and judgment.

Most people know that the Darden experience is demanding, but not all people know that the Darden experience is demanding, but not all ... why: extraordinary students, an unmatched level of faculty commitment ... all program set in the best business school facility anywhere, ... rated academic program with extensive and effec- ... port. Everyone contributes here ... group achievements. Our ... to each other's ... create

Darden changes the way you view your career, and what you can expect from your education. In fact, it cha...

Darden changes the way you view your career, and what you can expect from your education.
And it does so in ways no other school can match.
Darden focuses on your professional development.
It graduates business decision makers, men and women capable of exercising mature judgment on a w...
Darden alumni are:
• effective leaders as well as excellent managers,
• masters of a comprehensive core body of knowledge,
• people who value and excel at collaboration and the exchange of ideas,
• wise judges and decision makers,
• life-long learners and adapters, and
• well-rounded individuals—rather than narrow technicians—who act with social and ethic...

CHANGING THE WAY YOU THINK

SHOP TIL YOU DROP

Forget buyer beware, it's buyer be *empowered*.

There is an old saying, "Buyer beware," or in Latin, "Caveat emptor." Caveat emptor? Caveat schmaveat!

In today's retail environment, forget buyer beware. It's buyer be *empowered*.

From groceries and clothes to electronics and luxury items, consumers like to spend. With disposable incomes steadily climbing, this trend shows no signs of stopping. While this is certainly news that every vendor loves to hear, it has created an interesting environment in the business of doing business.

Consumers now have the ability to purchase almost whatever they can afford. What's more, digital advances have ensured that nothing is beyond the consumer's reach. From e-flowers to e-Mediterranean villas, consumers can buy virtually everything from the Internet's endless array of resources. These online vendors want— and need—business just as much as the boutique on the corner. Consumer empowerment means that all retailers—storefront and home page alike—are in fierce competition for attention and business.

As a result, virtues of customer service are now paramount. "The customer is always right" takes on new meaning, as each retailer must find and endorse a service that stands apart from everyone else's. Some offer no-hassle return policies, others free shipping, and still others boast no payments for a year. No matter what the hook, having one appears to be the best hope for reeling in customers.

The challenge takes on more dimensions. With customers buying more now than ever before, developing brand loyalty could not be more important. The role of marketing in consumer persuasion is at its zenith. It is not enough to stand out from the crowd, it's not even enough to get consumers to check out the merchandise. The ultimate challenge is to get them to check out—period—and to do so frequently and with many high-margin products.

The following examples of businesses have found the pulse of what consumers are seeking. From spaghetti sauce to shoes, these companies have successfully paired dynamic design with quality products to market themselves effectively. These companies not only make sales; they keep customers coming back for more.

ZEENZONE
AT CENTRAL DEPARTMENT STORE

To more accurately capture the the department's new-found character, Central sought a look that balanced fun with *savoir faire*, trendiness with sophistication, a sense of self with a sense of style. To convey its relevance to young Thais' lives, ZeenZone at Central was poised for a complete redesign of its interior architecture.

Although firmly rooted in ancient culture and Eastern philosophy, Bangkok, Thailand, on the surface at least, is becoming more and more Westernized. This is especially true of the city's younger generation which virtually worships things American. • A well-regarded establishment located in the Chidlom neighborhood of Bangkok, Thailand, Central Department Store was one of the capital's first modern shopping destinations. The flagship branch has long been viewed as a trusted resource but not one known for the trendy or cutting-edge. Its brand-new department named ZeenZone, unabashedly conceived to appeal to teens in both product and environment, has already changed that notion. • Central is more than a place to buy clothes. Indeed, today it's one of Thailand's most influential department stores—offering everything from a full grocery store to apparel,

Its bold, can't-miss design sets apart ZeenZone from the rest of the Bangkok, Thailand, department store. Structural columns wrapped in rainbow hues, for instance, punctuate the sales floor. Video screens are everywhere, adding to the high-energy, up-to-date atmosphere that's perfect for teens.

accessories, gifts and housewares. It is also an artistic creation. It is a place that encourages self-expression, not simply a location where merchandise occupies shelves. ZeenZone's made Central a destination, frequented as much for social interaction and "being seen" as it is for shopping or browsing.

To more accurately capture the essence of its character, Central needed to better communicate with its targeted audience of teens—a group who appreciates the excitement that accompanies living in the heart of Bangkok. The store had to

achieve a look that balanced fun with Western *savoir faire*, trendiness with sophistication, a sense of self with a sense of style. To convey its relevance to young Thais' lives, ZeenZone at Central was poised for a complete redesign of its interior architecture.

Beginning only with blueprints and preliminary concepts, an approach was developed that retained the store's basic space design but incorporated vibrant graphics through signage, displays, fixtures and furniture. Inviting, high-impact, design was key. As reflecting Asian preferences and attitudes was of paramount concern, colorful, fun and lively design was dominant. By addressing the store's overall architecture, a sense of place was created—an environment that truly represents the renewed, youthful spirit of the store. The task was not without its challenges however. This environment needed to be timeless. While fashions change and trends come and go, the graphics and interior design had to be appropriate for several years, requiring creative solutions that could transcend the role of short-lived displays and promotions.

An ice cream parlor and an Internet café within ZeenZone blur the line between shopping center and meeting place. Like teenagers in America, Thai kids enjoy hanging out with their friends at malls. These well placed "stations," set up for a refreshing milk shake or a surf of the Web, give

them a place to socialize in an environment designed just for them.

Fantasy and imagination underscore the department's graphics. A color-saturated illustration of a young girl, for instance, features a stylized lampshade for hair. A picture frame doubles as a suit on a cartoon-like young man; and a girl's shiny bracelet is actually a CD-ROM. Everyone has a different sense of style, yet everyone is stylish. ZeenZone recognizes this diversity—and encourages it.

In fact, style is evident in every space. Basic structural columns are transformed into larger-than-life displays that feature generic illustrations of the items offered in each department. Fluorescent colors and abstract patterns catch the eye. Couches shaped like perky flowers, for example,

Extremely versatile, the identity for ZeenZone allows for a wide range of fanciful illustration. Daisy-like flowers become eyeglasses on one young girl; a hat on another is suggestive of the Statue of Liberty's crown. All in all, graphics are unique and memorable, like those at ZeenZone's own ice cream parlor below.

Colorful, imaginative, and fun, at Central's ZeenZone, style is evident in every space. The overall environment is timeless, reflecting a playfully hip attitude appropriate for the young target audience.

are as much a part of the landscape as places to rest weary feet. Booth displays stand out with line art designs that are abstract and novel. The environmental graphic design strategy for the interior is also applied throughout ZeenZone's gifts and stationery department. As the store manufactures many of its own products, scaling down the bright and exciting graphics for notebooks, planners, cards, journals and other assorted notions provides a simple way for Central to ensure that its new look goes home with its customers. Shopping bags, as well, display this treatment and complete a high-quality, consistent look.

Central Department Stores had long been one of Thailand's leading retailers. It rightly earned a loyal, appreciative clientele through its wide variety of quality merchandise and convenient location. In order to endure, however, Central realized the need to reinvent itself—and begin to appeal to a new, younger generation. Free-form graphics combine with a creative color palette to communicate that—while Central Department store is a firmly established Thai institution—its ZeenZone is a fresh, hip, oasis for the younger set. Most importantly, it's become a destination that encourages teens to express who they are.

M Milk The challenge was to create new product packaging for milk that would make the wholesome beverage attractive to children and teenagers. A whimsical, yet keenly intelligent, design was chosen. This project proves that sometimes the best answer is the obvious one, but with a twist.

ure **in creating packaging for Pure, a small, blue-tinted glass bottle seemed a natural choice. The delicate curves and the light, airy color are reinforced by simple, clean typography and a clear label. These elements echo the simplicity of the product name.**

Barcode **A large plastic bottle was selected as the right container for a beverage targeting young, athletic men. Building on that foundation, bold but careful typography plays on the product name to complete the no-nonsense image.**

Delicious Works of Art

Museum of Cakes

Delicious Works of Art

Museum of Cakes

Scott Snelgrove • 1331 10th Street, NW • Washingto

Museum of Cakes It seemed obvious that the stationery and website for a company that creates beautiful, elegant—and edible—works of art should showcase its delectable products. Small examples of the company's handiwork are scattered around each page with the Museum of Cakes logo drawn to resemble tasty, multicolored icing.

SoHo Provisions This urban epicurie offers exotic foods from around the globe. As the company is ecologically minded, its logo and applications work to convey this message. Leaves and fruit are used frequently, giving the identity—and even the packaging—a "natural" feel. Various product brands, from bread crumbs to coffee, extend the company's identity.

Coquico The spirit and culture of Puerto Rico are captured in the unique plush toys created and sold by Coquico. To highlight the island's nocturnal tree frogs, the *coquí*, a simple, line-drawn logo is given character with large, bright eyes. The vibrant colors—rainforest green, ocean blue and papaya—celebrate Puerto Rico's tropical flavors.

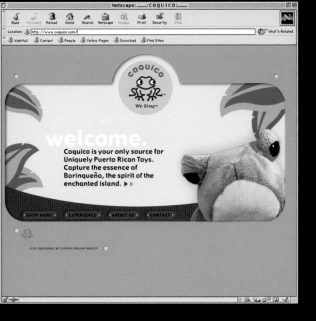

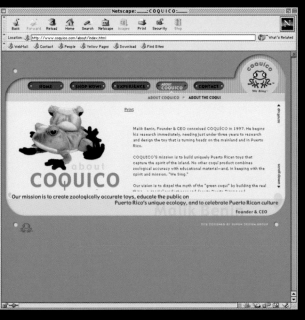

BEYOND SAFARI

wild life

SET INCLUDES: 12 SHE

BEYOND SAF

ld life

S: 12 SHEETS, 8 ENVELOPES

BEYOND SAFARI

Ever After This unique collection of stationery, greeting cards, posters and other notions captures the styles and spirits of the past and indulges them in a fresh and original light. Designed to evoke feelings of fantasy and nostalgia, Ever After rediscovers the magic of yesterday and brings a distinctive character to a diverse line of paper goods. A line of animal-print stationery appeals to a more "wild" audience.

claire's stores, inc.

ANNUAL REPORT
Fiscal Year Ended February 3, 2001

Claire's Stores **The leading mall-based retailer of popular-priced pre-teen and teen accessories, jewelry and apparel, Claire's is always aware of what's hot for its young demographic. The stores' annual report reflects this quality, while celebrating past performance and planning future goals and objectives.**

creating
individuals

Our customers know us. Our flagship concept, Claire's Accessories, enjoys 100% brand name recognition – an extraordinary advantage in a competitive retail climate. Claire's Accessories focuses on 7-12 year-old 'tweens, an age group that directly or indirectly accounts for $500 billion in household spending annually. For them, Claire's is a destination store, prominently located in the malls where they spend their time and their dollars. In fact, U.S. teens go to malls an average of 56 times a year, spending an average $20 per trip. And their numbers are growing.

Claire's pulls in young 'tweens with playful merchandise and an upbeat environment built to please – fun, young, inspired by the older teens and rock stars who are their fashion role models. By the millions, they know they can count on Claire's Accessories for the jewelry, accessories and cosmetics that speak to who they are now and who they want to be, all at an affordable price.

Claire's knows its market, 'tweens to twenties. Through the feedback we get on our website and monitoring the media, we learn who the celebs are that make them scream, the looks they like best and the things that melt their hearts. Our people track the latest trends, and work to keep our entire inventory one step ahead. Our in-store testing evaluates the market power of any item before it goes company-wide. From a puff of marabou on a picture frame to techno-bright socks, if it's new, we know it. If it's hot, we sell it. And in thousands of stores around the world, girls make a point of stopping by Claire's to buy it.

How strong is the concept? The Claire's Accessories formula, adapted over the years to changing demographics, is fresh and vibrant. It constitutes approximately 70% of our company's total sales, sets the style for our website, and serves as the foundation for our international growth. Like no other store, Claire's Accessories is the place where young girls find exactly what they're looking for: themselves.

2,027 | 3,032 | 3,025
'99 | '00 | '01

claire's store counts

Branding is a cornerstone of the Claire's Accessories current business strategy. To make more effective use of our franchise, we have our own private label cosmetics lines. By having one cohesive brand for Claire's and Afterthoughts, we can have a more impactful presentation and profit even more from the cosmetic category's strong market appeal.

Eileen Bonnie Schaefer
Vice Chairman,
Claire's Stores, Inc.

shaping
trends

With Claire's Accessories, our company polished the practice of focusing on a particular market segment, then penetrating it with merchandise, product mix and a store environment strategically geared to that market's mindset. But we haven't stopped there. We've gone on to apply that approach to different teen market segments, extending our reach to a broader spectrum of young girls... and even to the guys who live next door.

In the U.S. alone, our stores now appeal to every corner of the 79 million teens who make up Generation Y. Our Afterthoughts stores pick up the market where Claire's Accessories stores leave off, catering to young women from age 14 into their early twenties. And our Mr. Rags stores appeal to active teen boys with branded apparel and lifestyle departments that catch the wave of surf, skate and urban trends.

Located in popular malls in 31 states, Mr. Rags features the hardcore name brands active teens know, trust and want, along with a growing collection of private label apparel. With the urban-apparel market up to $6.8 billion for just the first nine months of last year, the stores are clearly in the right place at the right time. Mr. Rags takes the downtown look uptown – from New York to California, Albuquerque to Yorktown. Strong sales, more stores and a well received larger format prove the success of the Mr. Rags concept and the ability of merchandising and planning teams to identify fast-selling trends. We foresee further expansion of the chain into prime mall locations, profitably growing Mr. Rags from its current store base of 152 stores.

One reason for Mr. Rags' success is its authenticity. It not only has the look and apparel of the active teen life, but the equipment as well. In fact, it's one of the nation's largest mall-based hardgoods skateboard retailers. Inside a Mr. Rags store, it's easy for teens to picture themselves skating, surfing, wakeboarding, snowboarding – or just hanging out in streetwise style. Zapped with high-energy colors and a cool attitude, Mr. Rags is a place today's teens like to go, packed with the hip stuff they like to buy.

($ millions) | 54 | 87 | 114
1999 | 2000 | 2001

mr. rags sales growth

In 2001, Mr. Rags successfully tested a larger format store, and over the next fiscal year we remodel and expand stores to that format. Other changes ahead include a greater emphasis on private label products, accessories and seniors business. An increased use of the MMS allocation system is expected to improve inventory effectiveness and reduce markdowns.

Maria L. Schaefer
Vice Chairman,
Claire's Stores, Inc.

Narai Company Lighthearted illustrations in bold, lively colors were chosen for these pet food labels. Carefully planned color schemes solidify brand identity, while the "tail-end" of each can brings a surprise. The overall feeling is fun and engaging, entirely appropriate for the products and their furry admirers.

Gobey Gobey's full line of soy sauces are primarily sold in upscale gourmet shops. The bottles are given an elegant shape and an unusual size and are topped off with highly stylized labels and hang tags.

Green City Green City's Market and Cafe stocks only fresh, natural foods. Its identity, therefore, is designed with an upscale, health-conscious clientele in mind. It's made even more appealing with an earthy, organic look.

The Shops at National Place Contemporary illustrations are eye-catching and fun in these posters and bus stop ads created for one of downtown Washington's trendiest shopping centers. "Celebrate City Style" encourages professional men and women to explore the reinvigorated area's numerous boutiques and shops.

AQUA VITAE

LEFT TO RIGHT: Harris Chair Center, chair manufacturer; Andrew Paris, fashion designer; Aqua Vitae, beverage line; Charles Button Company, button manufacturer; Bugs and Bees, toymaker; Chesapeake Wine Company, wine bar and liquor store.

Apartment Zero Ready to debut its contemporary furniture and accessories in Washington, D.C., Apartment Zero needed a corporate identity for its grand opening. Vibrant, daring color paired with sleek, minimalist design reflects this shop's modern merchandise and sets it apart as a more hip option than typical furniture chains.

WHERE ART ORIGINATES

ROSENBAUM
FINE ART

Rosenbaum Fine Art A provider of fine art products to industry professionals, RFA needed a fresh ad campaign to appear in interior design and architectural magazines. The four ads subtly hint at glamorous and elegant models, but steadily avert the eye's focus to the paintings, producing an edgy—almost mysterious—concept that catches the attention of even the most discerning modern designer.

Wellsteads Wellsteads' emphasis on taste and nutrition, combined with its accessibility online and in stores, is a winning strategy amidst both fast-food and full-service restaurants. Eye-catching graphics distinguish it as a smart, healthy meal option for young, urban professionals.

Mystic Gardens This line of home fragrances radiates a magical and feminine appeal. Soft, muted colors stand out in comparison to the bold, deep tones that crowd store shelves. A drawing of a snail—with wings—emphasizes that this product offers something slightly different than the norm.

RIAL

RESEARCH

OPPORTUNITY

all about rosie

rosie

keep it r

"Put it before them briefly so they will
read it, **clearly** so they will appreciate it,
picturesquely so they will **remember**
it and, above all, accurately so they
will be guided by its **light**."
—JOSEPH PULITZER

"And a **free** T-shirt doesn't h

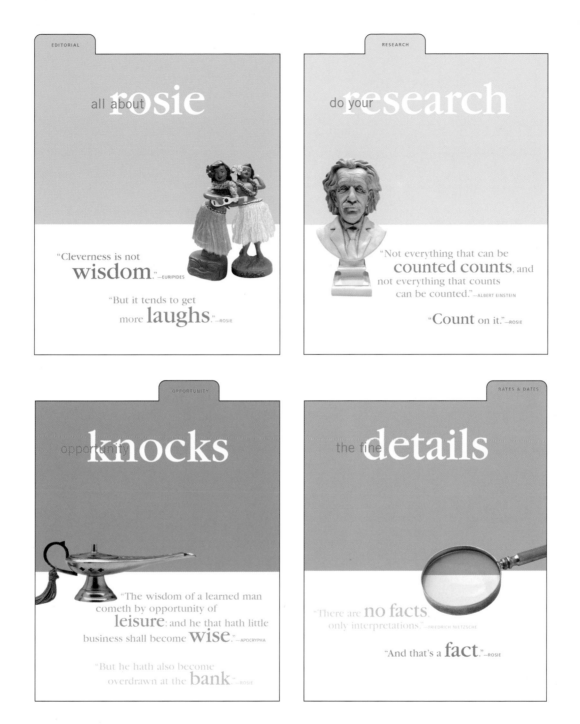

all about rosie

"Cleverness is not **wisdom**."—EURIPIDES

"But it tends to get more **laughs**."—ROSIE

do your research

"Not everything that can be **counted counts**, and not everything that counts can be counted."—ALBERT EINSTEIN

"**Count** on it."—ROSIE

opportunity **knocks**

"The wisdom of a learned man cometh by opportunity of **leisure**: and he that hath little business shall become **wise**."—APOCRYPHA

"But he hath also become overdrawn at the **bank**."—ROSIE

the fine **details**

"There are **no facts**, only interpretations."—FRIEDRICH NIETZSCHE

"And that's a **fact**."—ROSIE

Rosie Magazine **As unique as the publication's namesake, Rosie O'Donnell, this brightly hued media kit houses four loose pockets. Each features a quote from a respected figure along with a quick-witted retort from Rosie. A rubber toy chained to the spine clearly tags this kit with the personality of the celebrity publisher herself**

Host Marriott for Ronald Reagan National Airport **Four different templates were developed for the counter panels of the airport's food area, allowing each tenant to choose the look it favored. These were then customized to each vendor's color scheme and food selection, ensuring all a unique look that fit within the overall aesthetic.**

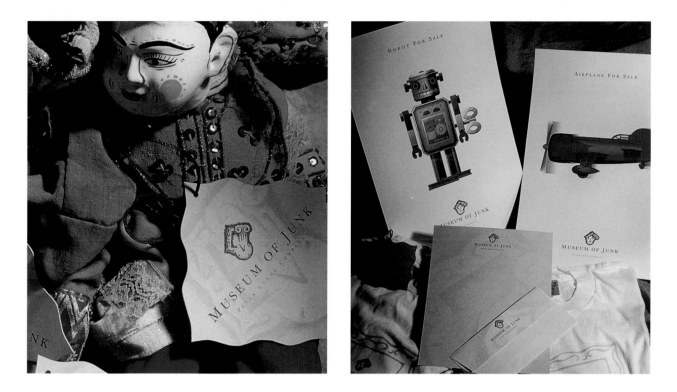

Museum of Junk This unique store is a playful cross between a museum and a junk shop, where customers can buy antique treasures, whimsical collectibles or inexpensive replicas. The logo, applied to everything from shopping bags to a website, fuses three icons into one, conveying nostalgia, art and classicism in a single image. The result is a feeling that is at once old and new.

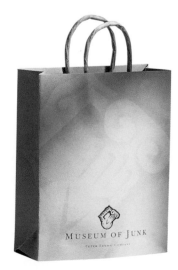

Fresh Market In the labeling system for this line of pre-cut, ready-to-cook produce, the classic, softer lines are intended to appeal to urbane, health-conscious consumers. The approach revitalizes the ubiquitous plastic packaging system.

CSS Cosmetics Packaging design for two very different products—Pacifika body lotion and Perfect Hair styling cream—each fits its own market in ways which differentiate it from competing brands. An airy poppy suggests the subtle floral essence of one while the retro style of the other is appropriate for men seeking 1950s-like sleekness.

Museum of Shoes This shoe store showcases footwear spotted on some of today's biggest celebrities, and sells reproductions of these fashions as well as other popular shoe brands. The Museum's initials create a column in the elegant, playful mark that elevates shoes to—according to some—their rightful place in society. Packaging and signage expand on the identity established with the logo.

SkinVestment A line of cooling packs that help heal cuts, bumps and bruises, SkinVestment's Boo Boo Buddy products perfect the distinct child-focused marketing approach. Branded as "My Boo Boo Buddy" items, the colorful and cheerful products drive children's desire to have their own.

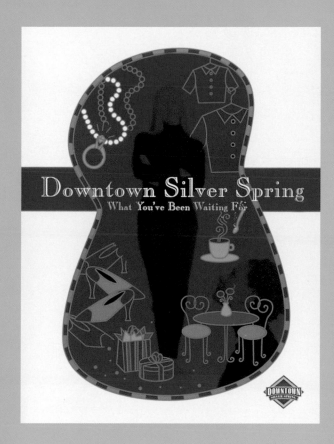

The Peterson Companies Encouraging retailers to lease space in the exciting and diverse Downtown Silver Spring (Maryland), this brochure's lively color and carefree illustration communicate that Silver Spring is a dynamic community and a vibrant hub of shops, restaurants and entertainment venues that just can't be passed up.

complete packages, including sides and dessert
priced per person, minimum 8 people

IT'S A WRAP

$10.99 per person

A trio of our Chef's choice of Signature Wraps. Your choice of 2 side salads. Includes an assortment of Signature cookies, brownies and dessert bars.

THE AMERICAN

$12.99 per person

All natural Virginia Baked Ham, Smoked Turkey, Roast Beef, Cheddar & Provolone Cheese with lettuce, tomato, onions, pickles, olives, sliced bread, Chipotle Mayonnaise, Dijon mustard & canola mayonnaise. Your choice of 2 side salads. Includes an assortment of Signature cookies, brownies and dessert bars.

THE ROMAN

$11.99 per person

Our Signature Caesar Dressing makes this salad special—grilled chicken with crisp romaine lettuce, tomato, shredded Parmesan cheese and home-made croutons. Comes with assorted rolls, fruit salad and an assortment of Signature cookies, brownies and dessert bars. Substitute grilled salmon for chicken, add $2.00 per person.

THE GREEK

$9.99 per person

A classic Greek salad with cucumbers, artichokes, tomatoes, onion, chickpeas and feta cheese with our Mediterranean Vinaigrette. We include hummus and pita bread, fruit salad and an assortment of Signature cookies, brownies and dessert bars. Add grilled chicken $2.00 per person. Add shrimp $4.00 per person.

THE ITALIAN

$14.99 per person

All natural Salami, Sopressata, Prosciutto, Provolone cheese, Marinated Fresh Mozzarella, marinated artichokes and olives. Served with lettuce, tomato & crusty bread with Saffron Aioli & Tapenade to spread. Accompanied by Grilled Vegetable Pasta and an assortment of Signature cookies, brownies and dessert bars.

SIGNATURE COOKIES & BARS

Whole Foods The catering menu for this upscale grocery store showcases exactly what this chain is recognized for—high-quality prepared foods made with only the choicest and freshest ingredients. It was important not to "overdesign" this piece so that the foods could speak for themselves.

WE THE PEOPLE

How often do we think about who's
keeping the country on track?

It seems that in the blink of an eye, 300 million people will be living in the United States. As everyone goes about their day-to-day lives, how often—or rarely—do they stop to think about the various organizations keeping the country on track?

Governmental departments and agencies operate on behalf of every person in the U.S. They are the organizations that—with a delicate and almost imperceptible hand—regulate the nation and represent everyone's interests. No small task, they strive to allow all Americans access to shelter, transportation, jobs and education. They ensure the safety of foods, medicines and national borders. They promote the advancement of the country nationally, internationally and in the broad expanses of space.

What is most remarkable about these organizations is the diversity of people they serve. The American "melting pot" is well-stirred with a wide variety of ethnic backgrounds, races and occupations. The challenge faced by governmental agencies and chartered organizations is to find the best avenue by which to communicate with each of these people, while considering the sometimes vast differences in their individual lives and needs.

Similar to traditional businesses, governmental departments and agencies must identify their key target audiences and then implement strategies designed to reach each one effectively. In this way, they efficiently communicate their messages. Unlike businesses, however, they generally do not face competition from industry rivals. Nor do they confront the demands of meeting revenue targets or retaining loyal buyers. Rather, these organizations' clients are the general public, and the competition they face is for attention and support.

Ultimately, governmental organizations must develop identities that allow them to be easily and clearly recognized. In the flurry of today's bustling society, they must create a space both to communicate their services and convey their utility as a resource. With such a broad and diverse audience—everyone—these identities must be user-friendly and accessible.

The governmental organizations featured in the next pages successfully employ clear and strong design techniques in their public communication efforts. As a result, they not only show service and capability, they display pride in the U.S. and the rights and liberties on which the country was founded.

UNITED STATES POSTAL SERVICE

A new generation of commemorative stamp souvenirs provides the United States Postal Service with educational and enjoyable products that communicate with the organization's key audience: everyone.

Postmaster General John Wanamaker caused quite a disturbance in 1893 when he issued the nation's first commemorative postage stamps. Even a congressional joint resolution protested the stamps as "unnecessary," but Wanamaker insisted the series would be a success. • The controversial first commemorative edition was entitled "Columbian Exposition." The series of 115 stamps honored the 400th anniversary of Christopher Columbus's 1492 voyage to the New World. Critics quickly pointed out discrepancies in the artwork on the one- and two-cent stamps, and condemned the two-, three-, four- and five-dollar values as useless for sending packages in that day and age. • To show his confidence in the edition's success, Postmaster General Wanamaker spent $10,000 of his own money and bought 5,000 of the two-dollar stamps, then stored them in his safe as an investment. As Wanamaker had expected, the stamps'

GREENBAY

VINCE

incent Thomas Lombardi, born in
1913, is one of the most successful
football coaches ever. His winning
percentage, .740, is listed in the 1996
Guinness Book of Records. Lombardi
played football as a student at Fordham
University in 1936-38.
After spending some
time coaching high
school and college
teams, he entered
professional football,
assuming command of the Green Bay
Packers in 1959, at the age of 46.
With Green Bay, Lombardi was a
catalyst for a dramatic reversal of fortune;
though they had not had a winning
season in 11 years, their record

L

Lombo
Their
was
dis
fr

U.S. POSTAL SERVICE

LEGENDS
OF
FOOTBALL

A NOSTALGIC TRIBUTE
TO FOUR OF THE GRIDIRON'S
GREATEST COACHES

Legends of Football and American Comic Classics are two of the many commemorative stamp souvenirs developed for the U.S. Postal Service. Whether through dramatic color photographs or vibrant cartoon icons, each souvenir tells a story.

release created a sensation as hundreds of collectors and customers rushed to purchase them. In all, two billion commemorative Columbus stamps were sold, for 40 million dollars. The stamps, still in the safe when Wanamaker died in 1926, were valued at $4.50 each.

Today's more recent commemorative stamps—honoring Georgia O'Keeffe, Marilyn Monroe or American Indian dances, to name a few—create a seemingly insatiable demand for the unique souvenir products that accompany them. As the United States Postal Service is a resource for every American and a constant figure in the public eye—now more than ever—its products need to be especially user-friendly and accessible.

The stamps' subjects were used as stylistic and conceptual starting points in the development of many such souvenirs. Eye-catching graphics, innovative layouts, vivid color and engaging

copy contribute to the value and novelty of the new editions. Elements such as die-cuts and foldouts add a special flair, as each series is distinguished by a range of subject matter so broad that it brings its own particular challenges and rewards.

Souvenirs for the Postal Service take on diverse formats, but each houses a single stamp or stamp set commemorating a particular person, culture or event with a first-day-of-issue cancellation. A brief history of the featured subject is included.

Rudolf Valentino, Buster Keaton, Charlie Chaplin and Clara Bow are among the 10 stars from yesteryear whose talent and celebrity are honored by a set of commemorative stamps. Richly designed with hundreds of photos and narrated with stimulating copy, the commemorative stamps and corresponding book, *Legends of the Silent Screen,* portray an era when Hollywood really was a

Elements such as die-cuts and foldouts add a special flair to each souvenir. ABOVE: **Classic American Aircraft** OPPOSITE, LEFT TO RIGHT: **Jazz Musicians, Centennial Olympic Games, Hollywood Monster Classics, Civil War.**

shining city on a hill. Affixed to the inside of the book is a genuine block of all 10 postage stamps, each illustrated by the well-known cartoonist Al Hirschfeld.

American Comic Classics celebrates the 100th anniversary of the comic strip with 20 of the most beloved characters from the first 50 years of the art form. Vibrantly colored cartoons of each character—like Blondie, Popeye and Flash Gordon—are interspersed with little-known information about the strips and their artists. The playful, upbeat pages of the book look like they were torn right from the comics. A block of all 20 commemorative stamps is mounted on the inside cover, making the edition a true collector's item.

A series of posters was the chosen medium for the Postal Service's Pro-Cycling Team. Every design promotes a race in a different city and features active illustrations of speeding cyclists superimposed onto background images specific to that city. Affixed to each poster is a genuine U.S. postage stamp, cancelled on the day of the race. Some of the posters are signed by Pro-Cycling Team members, ensuring each element of the series is a valuable—and memorable—piece for collectors.

Two different products were created for the 1996 Centennial Modern Olympic Games in Atlanta. Twenty ready-to-mail perforated postcards are bound into a booklet. Each features a different full-bleed illustration of the Olympic athletes who appear on the stamps.

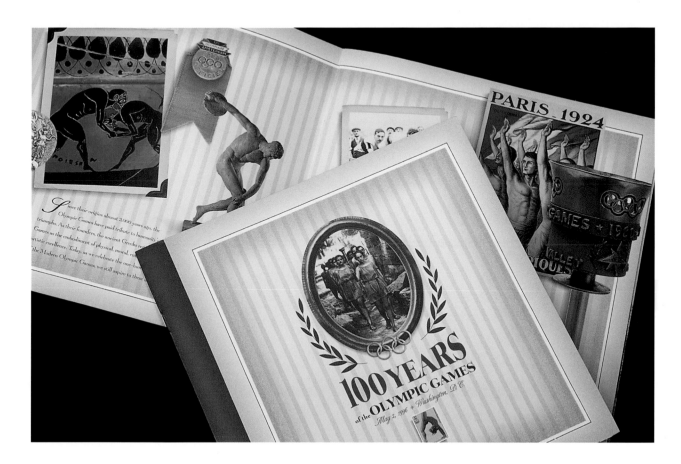

Some people and events leave indelible marks in American history. Artist Georgia O'Keeffe and the Olympic Games are remembered with stamps and commemorative pieces that are richly illustrated and magnificently narrated.

Featuring strong primary colors and impressive physiques in motion, the postcard booklet celebrates a century of the modern Olympic Games with a look back at some of the its finest moments.

These commemorative stamp souvenirs join with many other subjects, including James Dean, Jazz Musicians, the Boston Marathon and the Civil War, in establishing a group of tangible, compelling keepsakes that celebrate the truly fascinating aspects of history that have shaped the United States. With these souvenirs, the Postal Service has developed a new generation of educational and enjoyable products that communicate with the organization's key audience: everyone interested in Americana.

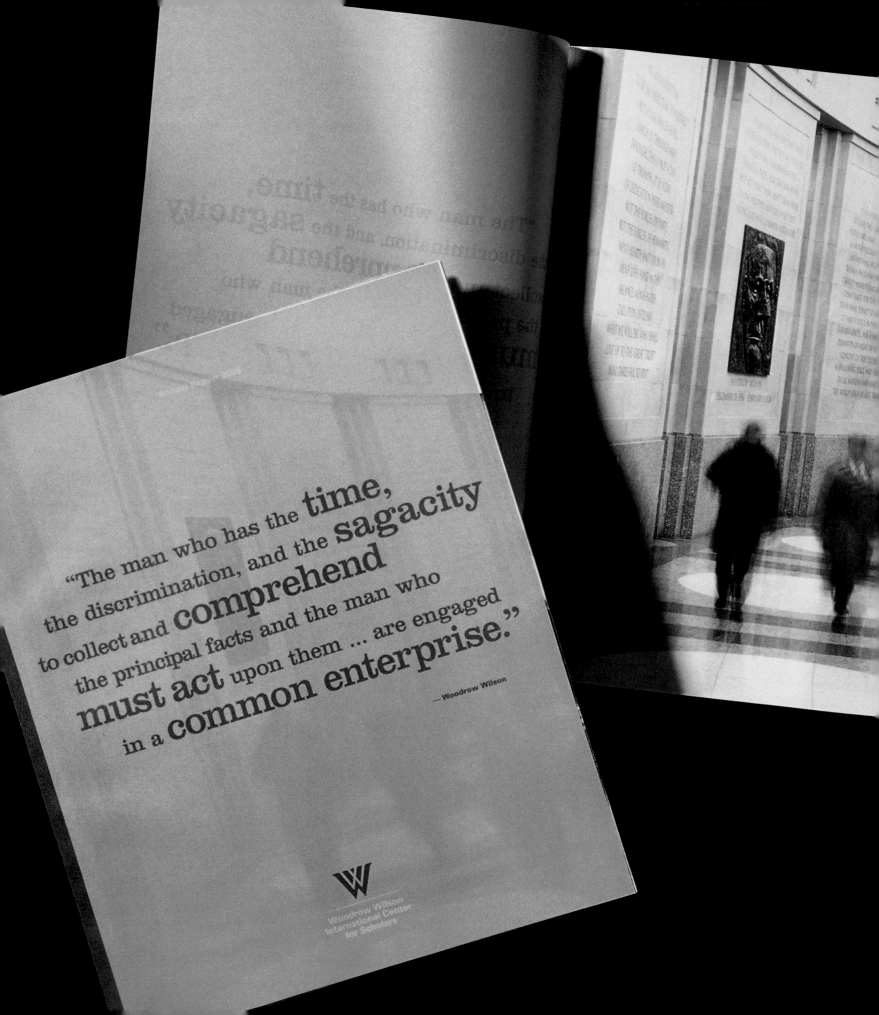

"The man who has the time, the discrimination, and the sagacity to collect and comprehend the principal facts and the man who must act upon them ... are engaged in a common enterprise."

— Woodrow Wilson

Woodrow Wilson International Center for Scholars An institution dedicated to uniting the worlds of policy and scholarship, the Woodrow Wilson Center wanted to attract a new generation of business leaders—the future policymakers of the world. A sophisticated, less formal branding identity was applied to its annual report, uniting all its departments and programs around one cohesive look.

This brochure promotes the American Folk Life Center at the U.S. Library of Congress, an extensive archive chronicling American folk culture. A diverse mix of photographs from these archives was used behind the letterforms of the Center's name. This suggests the breadth of the collection and its relevance to Americans' lives today.

What is American Folklife?

American folklife includes:

- Songs
- Stories
- Jokes and riddles
- Children's games
- Family recipes and food traditions
- Holiday customs
- Community celebrations
- Religious festivals
- Dance
- Vernacular architecture
- Occupational skills and lore
- Quilts, wood carvings, basketry, and other crafts

"Folklore is the lips of people of all colors, races, and creeds. It is in their minds and in their hearts. In its rich folklife, America has given expression to the creative urge through its songs and its dances, its arts and its crafts, and through the handiwork of all that man himself has fashioned."

— Wayland Hand, professor of folklore, founding member, American Folklife Center Board of Trustees

For nearly everyone, the experience of folklife begins at home, where family members prepare food, tell stories, play music, play games, and celebrate the holidays. But folklife can be found in virtually all groups of people who come together regularly for a common purpose.

American folklife is "the traditional expressive culture shared within the various groups in the United States: familial, ethnic, occupational, religious, regional; expressive culture includes a wide range of creative and symbolic forms such as custom, belief, technical skill, language, literature, art, architecture, music, play, dance, drama, ritual, pageantry, handicraft; these expressions are mostly without benefit of formal instruction or institutional direction."

The American Folklife Preservation Act of 1976

"Folklore is the boiled-down juice, or potlikker, of human beings."
— Zora Neale Hurston, folklorist

LEFT TO RIGHT: United States Department of Agriculture, federal agricultural agency; Washington, D.C.: The American Experience, city tourism and promotional program; United States Botanic Garden, national garden and museum; United States Patent and Trademark Office, federal agency for industrial and technological progress; United States Postal Service, "Celebrate the Century" 100-year stamp retrospective; Woodrow Wilson International Center for Scholars, public affairs and scholarship institution.

Smithsonian Institution A traveling exhibition commemorating the Institution's 150th anniversary, America's Smithsonian contains a selection of the museum's most treasured objects. The familiar Smithsonian sunburst icon is split into four parts, each often filled with a tightly cropped artifact image.

United States Department of Energy A user-friendly, informative website that appeals to consumers as well as scientists and researchers, energy.gov is a gateway to a wealth of information about energy and how it affects every American. Intuitive navigation and comfortable design succeed in reintroducing the Department of Energy as a truly consumer-focused organization.

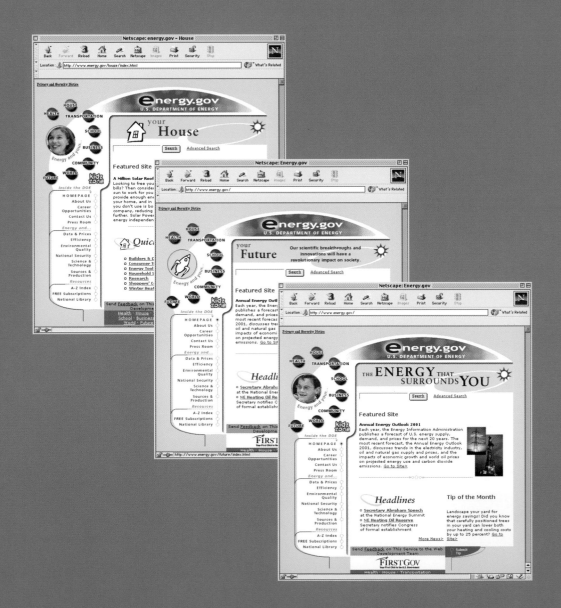

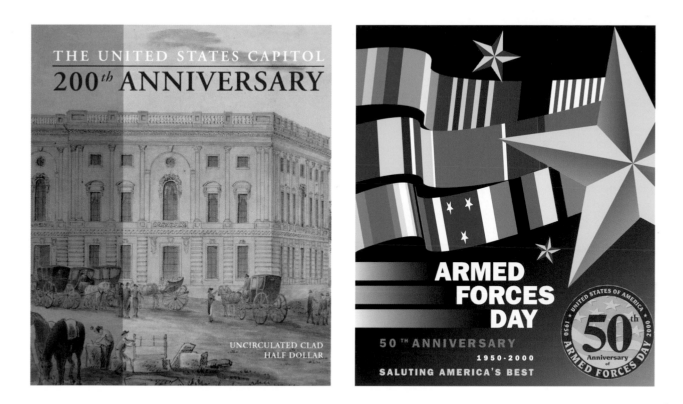

United States Treasury, Department of the Mint: This direct marketing brochure cover established the look for an entire campaign promoting three coins commemorating the 200th anniversary of the U.S. Capitol building; **United States Department of Defense:** Marking the 50th anniversary of Armed Forces Day, this piece pays tribute to the role the Department plays in safeguarding our nation; **United States Marine Band:** Packaging and collateral were created for a CD-ROM containing music from the President's own marching band.

NATIONAL MEDIATION BOARD
2000 Annual Performance Report
For the Fiscal Year Ending September 30, 2000

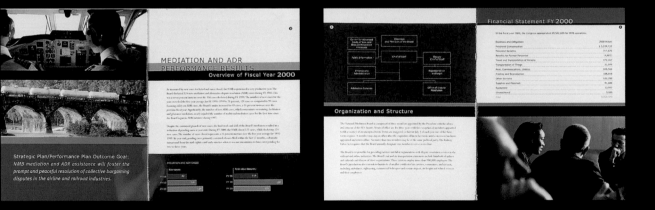

National Mediation Board The NMB arbitrates labor and union disputes in the airline and railroad industries. Rather than send a typical performance report to its government audiences, it wanted to develop a professional, sophisticated aware-ness piece that would communicate its capabilities. Colorful photos of the air